ARIZONA HIDEAWAYS

Stories and Photos by

Thelma Heatwole

author of

Ghost Towns & Historical Haunts in Arizona
Arizona—Off the Beaten Path!

Golden West Publishers

Acknowledgment

Articles about Benson, Bisbee, Bullhead City, Clifton, Cochise, Fredonia, Jerome, Patagonia, Quartzsite, Ramsey Canyon and Strawberry which have appeared in the *Arizona Republic* 1980-1985 are copyright by Phoenix Newspapers, Inc. and reprinted with their permission.

FRONT COVER... The delightful hideaway at Hannagan Meadow

Front and back cover design and maps by Bruce Robert Fischer

Physical hazards may be encountered in visiting areas of ARIZONA HIDEAWAYS, particularly old mining localities. Land ownerships and road conditions change over the years. Readers should take proper precautions and make local inquiries, as author and publishers cannot accept responsibility for such matters.

```
Library of Congress Cataloging-in-Publication Data

Heatwole, Thelma,
    Arizona hideaways.

    Includes index.
    1. Arizona--Description and travel--Guide-
books. I. Title.
F809.3.H395  1986      917.91'0453      86-18422
ISBN 0-914846-25-6
```

Printed in the United States of America

Copyright ©1986 by Thelma Renick Heatwole. All rights reserved. This book, or any portion thereof, may not be reproduced in any form, except for review purposes, without the written permission of the publisher.

Golden West Publishers
4113 N. Longview Ave.
Phoenix, AZ 85014, USA

Dedication

*This book is dedicated
to my husband Don
and our sons Bruce and David
for their support and enthusiasm—
always.*

PRECAUTIONS:

Exploring Arizona's vastness, scenic beauty and small towns calls for cautions.

- Some areas are pocked with mines, potholes, old wells. Don't forget the desert washes that can flood and quicksand that may lurk in riverbeds, streams and water holes.
- Keep an eye out for snakes and other denizens of the remote country.
- Bubonic plague has been found in wild animals, such as rodents, rabbits, coyotes in several portions of Arizona, according to the state Department of Health Services. Craig Levy, of the department's Disease Control Division, said the plague can be transmitted to humans by fleas that have fed on infected animals.
- Gas, food, water and first-aid supplies must be sufficient for travel destinations.

Remains of Army wagon near doctor's quarters at Fort Verde State Historic Park

CONTENTS

Precautions 4

Introduction 6

North Central (map) 8
    Fredonia 9
    Page 12
    Cameron 15
    Williams 18
    Ash Fork 21
    Seligman 24

Northeast (map) 26
    Second Mesa 27
    Window Rock 29
    Chambers 33
    St. Johns 36
    Snowflake 38
    Heber 41

East (map) 43
    Alpine 44
    Hannagan Meadow 46
    Honeymoon 48
    Morenci 51
    Clifton 53
    Superior 57
    Kearny 60
    Mammoth 63

Southeast (map) 65
    Bowie 66
    Cochise 69
    Benson 72
    Bisbee 76
    Ramsey Canyon 80
    Patagonia 83

Southwest (map) 86
    Gila Bend 87
    Ajo 90

West (map) 95
    Wickenburg 96
    Wikieup 99
    Bullhead City 101
    Parker 103
    Quartzsite 106

Mid-Central (map) 109
    Strawberry 110
    Camp Verde 113
    Cottonwood 116
    Jerome 119
    Mayer 121

Index 125

Introduction

Most travelers who spend the night on the road choose larger towns, but some of the state's lesser-known little towns offer a special blend of atmosphere, hospitality and history.

How many travelers, for instance, have spent the night—or even thought of it—in Cochise? Or Mammoth? Or Quartzsite?

Probably few people realize that one can spend the night at Wikieup. Most people whiz through the place enroute to Kingman and Las Vegas without batting an eye. If they stop, it's probably for a quick cup of coffee.

Small towns may be worth a longer encounter.

In Quartzsite, there may be a "tailgate" sale on a cooler-weather weekend. Prize finds on a stop included an old political campaign button and turquoise earrings. Besides, the people were friendly.

In some places, such as St. Johns, there are excellent museums. Townspeople are understandably proud of their museums and eager to share their histories.

At Seligman, sunset was casting its last pink rays, and diners at The Brass Cart could see the lights signalling the Black Cat Bar across the street.

Towns like Snowflake and Fredonia offer old shade trees and broad main streets. Snowflake is noted for its historic houses.

Small towns are quiet places. Some have volunteer firefighters and visitors may hear the siren wail. And, many little towns have the first letter in their name painted on a mountain that overlooks the town. That bespeaks of community pride.

Some towns have chambers of commerce. The C of C may be headed by a man in his business place, but it is still a source of information.

And down in southern Arizona, there's Benson and Bowie and Patagonia, each with its own proud heritage.

History is big, too, in Camp Verde, where the old Clear Creek Church has been restored through a very active historical society. Fort Verde State Historical Park is a must to see.

In Kearny, the spirit of Gen. Stephen Watts Kearny, of U.S. Army fame, still pervades. His legendary life is heralded in a bronze plaque along Main Street.

Arizona's little towns do invite exploring. And many offer outstanding area scenery. We always carry picnic fare to eat in scenic places.

Arizona's little towns, though, do invite exploring.

Granted an overnight stay does not give visitors in-depth knowledge of the place. But travelers can gain at least a casual viewpoint, an on-the-spot look by spending the night in the little towns.

One must, of course, have overnight accommodations for the hideaway adventures. Do not expect to stay in a Hilton-type motel. Accommodations usually are not plush, though most places we found were clean and comfortable. Since some small town lodgings have no television or radio, take along a good book or plan to gain some extra sleep.

Most motels are priced lower than in larger places. A motel in Superior, for instance, was an unbelievable $15 for the night. But, that was in 1983.

And another thing. There is often the opportunity to buy an unusual item for the home.

I did not keep a tally, but I can recall a clever chandelier from an antique shop in Mayer. It now adorns the family room.

Then there is the plant holder, handpainted on all sides by an artist I met in Bowie. And, in Ashfork, an artist painted bits of flagstone for clever items of room decor.

And so it goes. One can never tell what surprise little towns may hold.

These stories are what visitors may observe or want to know for an overnight or longer visit.

Learn as much as you can about the town. You may never go that way again—or, you may return again and again.

No two towns are alike. Each has its own personality.

That's the fun of visiting Arizona's hideaways!

8 Map of North Central Arizona

REMOTE FREDONIA
rich in history!

A quiet place—small, with a white "F" emblazoned on a redrock mountain overlooking the town, Fredonia is reminiscent of little towns of yesteryear.

A wailing fire siren bespoke of concerned volunteers in this town that incorporated in 1956.

Streets must be named for townspeople past or present. On Hortt Street, a tall white house obviously old but well cared for, adds to the homey character. The town's residential areas boast both old and newer houses, schools, a park with pool.

In a January 1983 visit, old trees that shade the town's broad main street in the summer were leafless, the limbs quivering nakedly in a stiff breeze.

Nedra's Cafe was a warm refuge from the cold, and dining there offered a respite from the wind that whipped about outside.

Elsewhere, in quarters in a school building, Caroline Carlley, 83, town librarian, helped patrons in the small but cozy library where shelves groaned with books.

The town was in the process of getting a library of its own, and Carlley, who came here 21 years ago as a teacher, anticipated that

Steamboat Rock on the Arizona Strip

School bell fronts Fredonia School

day.

Fredonia is tucked in a remote area of the Arizona Strip Country, along U.S. Alt. 89, seven miles from Kanab, Utah, where strong neighborly ties exist.

The community neared the centennial of its 1885 founding. Historians say the place was called Stewart and Union before Erastus Snow, one of the 12 apostles of the Latter Day Saints Church, urged that the name be Fredonia, which, some say, means "free women."

Arizona Place Names notes that in 1885 a number of Mormon families left Utah seeking freedom from efforts to suppress polygamy.

In the Fredonia Library's book of town history, a citizen disputed the claim. "The statement is not true," the writer noted, "as only one of the seven pioneers of Fredonia had more than one wife . . .."

A town official reported that in 1980 the census was 1075.

In 1983, the town had a woman mayor, woman court clerk-magistrate and three women on the school board. The town, without a newspaper of its own, is served by three periodicals. Its former newspaper, **The Arizona Strip Teaser,** produced by women, was no longer publishing.

Kaibab Industries, a lumber operation, was the town's number one industry, employing at times as many as 600. The North Kaibab Ranger Station, a U.S. flag flying from its towering pole, employs between 40 and 100 workers, depending on the season.

Among facilities in the town were a bank, established here in

1982, and three motels. Many people travel the short distance to Kanab, a larger town, for dining and shopping. The Territorial Inn, Kanab, offered good food and atmosphere.

Pipe Springs National Monument, an area attraction 14 miles away, is in the northeast extremity of Mohave County. Its waters that break through the surface and create an oasis setting were known by long ago Indians and Spanish explorers.

The first Mormons to use the springs were missionaries with Jacob Hamblin the group leader.

In 1868, the place became a military headquarters, and still later Mormon Church leader Brigham Young decided a fort should be built there for the convenience and safety of those who lived there. It became a national monument by proclamation of President Harding in 1923.

Pipe Springs with its quaint museum and glance into history is well worth a visit.

Pipe Springs National Monument—a short drive from Fredonia

Page offers variety of shopping areas

PAGE
a recent page in Arizona history!

A visit in this town, situated on a mesa with a view of Glen Canyon Dam and its beautiful man-made Lake Powell, can add a novel page to Arizona travel adventures.

One of Arizona's newest communities, Page celebrated its quarter-century anniversary in April 1982.

The town began as a housing camp during construction of the famed dam along the Colorado River in a far recess of Arizona, just south of the Utah border.

Its main magnet now for travelers is proximity to Lake Powell that mirrors the blue sky and salmon-pink rock formations in myriad shapes and monoliths. Scenic flights take off at Page, and on the lake, cruises and fishing are big.

Professionally arranged cruises may be boarded at marinas, including Wahweap. A favorite destination is the majestic Rainbow Bridge. There are private boats, but boaters should be knowledgeable of the vast lake and its many recesses.

The community with its relatively short history was founded in 1957 by the U.S. Bureau of Reclamation. The town was named for John C. Page, a commissioner of the Bureau of Reclamation during FDR's administration.

Arizona Republic files indicate the town was under administration of the bureau 16 years. The city officially was declared incorporated on March 1, 1975.

The town today offers numerous motels and restaurants, and its shopping areas contain a variety of stores, including a Babbitt's Supermarket and Department Store.

The dinner menu at "The Old West" set the tone of the restaurant. A folksy statement said: "Our whole desire is to make this the most enjoyable evening you have ever spent away from home."

The town, besides its commercial and residential areas, includes modern schools, a radio station, two newspapers and probably a dozen churches.

Important segment of the Page scenario is the Navajo coal-fired generating station, billed as Arizona's largest generating station. Six years in the making at a construction cost of $659 million, the project uses water from Lake Powell in its operation.

The station is on the Navajo Indian Reservation, 4½ miles southeast of downtown Page. With about 800 full-time employees working at the plant, plus up to 400 additional temporary employees, the project is an important segment of Page economy.

The plant-owned Black Mesa and Lake Powell Railroad delivers coal to the station from Kayenta Mines on the Black Mesa, a 160-mile round trip. The BM&LP is an electrically-fueled system.

Glen Canyon Dam is billed as the second highest concrete dam in the nation. 'Tis said there is enough concrete in Glen Canyon Dam to pave a highway from Phoenix to Chicago, four inches thick and four lanes across.

Lake Powell began forming in September 1963, the day the dam

Navajo Project Generating Station marks Page skyline

was finished.

Travel to Page is part of the fun. Interstate 40 is left beyond Flagstaff to head north on U.S. 89 and into Navajo Indian country. Motoring along the Painted Desert Scenic Drive (still on 89) is a jostling but colorful extravaganza. The mauves and pink scenic scapes through Echo Cliffs are fascinating.

Roadside stands where Indian jewelry is sold were mostly vacant on a cold January day. Occasional hogan-type homes and flocks of sheep add quaint notes.

Glen Canyon Bridge spans Colorado River in rugged rock formation setting

Lake Powell near Wahweap Marina

CAMERON TRADING POST
on the Little Colorado River

The idea developed rather suddenly.

We were traveling along U.S. Highway 89 through Navajo Land with its dramatic natural colors and aura of peace.

Why not spend the night at Cameron Trading Post?

The idea started jelling over a bowl of vegetable soup in the trading post dining room. Navajo rugs adorned the walls. Curtains were emblazoned with Kachina doll motifs. Colorful paintings, Indian pottery, sand paintings, moccasins—all lent an Indian country atmosphere.

Inquiring about accommodations, we found a newer lodge building with balcony overlooking the winding Little Colorado River with suspension bridge and the colorful rock hills of the Painted Desert.

We made reservations to spend the night in the Navajo Lodge two nights later. Our stay in Navajoland proved an interesting stanza.

Cameron (originally Tanner's Crossing), according to an historical marker near the suspension bridge, "is named for one of Arizona's first U.S. Senators (Ralph Cameron), a pioneer in the development of trails and copper mines in the Grand Canyon. Near here was the site of Tanner's Crossing of the Little Colorado River on the Mormon Trail from Utah via Lee's Ferry to settlements in Arizona and Mexico."

Arizona Place Names notes that "in 1911 when the bridge across the Little Colorado River was built, Scott Preston, a Navajo, had a store where Cameron is today. In the same year Hubert Richardson began a settlement and named it for the U.S. Senator Cameron, last territorial delegate for Arizona to the U.S. Congress."

Joe Atkinson, Cameron Trading Post owner, verified Richardson's connection with the post starting in 1911. He said the first section of the hotel was started in 1916 with the Zuni and Hopi sections built in the 1920s and 1930s, respectively. The Navajo section was rebuilt in 1977 after a fire.

Atkinson, owner since August 1985, owns the trading post and buildings that are on a 112-acre plot of deeded land. Richardson, Atkinson said, quit operating the business in 1966.

In a visit in 1983, our room was nicely furnished, including color cable television. (The winter rate was $20.55 for one bed, two

Curious and hungry travelers often stop at trading post in Indian country

Navajo part of lodge provides rest for weary travelers

16   CAMERON (North Central Arizona)

people.)

Zane Gray, we were told, spent many nights at the motel and even mentioned the trading post in his books.

An employee said that during heavy travel seasons, the hotel is full every night. Tour groups arrive frequently by the bus load.

The trading post has its own water and sewer system. Indians living in the area often come to the trading post for water.

Cameron has several churches, a post office, school for primary through third grade (other students are bussed to Tuba City), a mini mart, service stations, and pockets of residential areas.

Oldtimers can remember that when sheep flocks crossed the narrow suspension bridge for one-way traffic, the sheep crossed while cars waited. In the 1950s, the original bridge over the Little Colorado River (that is said to contain pockets of quick silver) was condemned and a new, wider bridge was constructed.

The post dining room on a January evening was relatively quiet. Prices were modest. Menu temptations included a Cameron steak and roast pork. Navajo tacos and Indian fry bread are popular items.

After browsing and buying at the trading post at night, there was ample television. A night in the total quiet of the trading post motel did offer a change of pace. A welcome one.

Old suspension bridge over the Little Colorado River bespeaks of bygone days

WILLIAMS
"gateway to the Grand Canyon"

The spirit of Old Bill Williams lives on. Townspeople see to that. The Bill Williams tributes go on and on.

The city is named for William Sherley Williams, a colorful mountaineer, trapper and guide who died in 1849.

The main drag through town, with its succession of restaurants, Indian craft shops, motels and sundry businesses, is called Bill Williams Avenue.

The town snuggles in the lap of Bill Williams Mountain which provides a colorful backdrop for the place. There is also a Bill Williams River.

The Bill Williams Mountain Men annually attract publicity. They organized in 1953 to help perpetuate the lore and romance of the mountain men of old.

Perhaps, capping the accolades to the mountain men is the Bill Williams Monument, a bronze statue said to be 8½ feet in height and weighing 1000 pounds. It was installed in 1980 in the city park alongside Bill Williams Avenue. Tourists pause to aim their cameras at the statue and read the lengthy inscription. The rugged trapper, according to the memorial, first visited the site of Williams in 1826. Some claim he spent the 1832-33 winter in the area.

The tributes and nostalgia combine to set the aura of the town. But, Williams, basking in a valley in the Kaibab Forest, has another title. Today, the Williams-Grand Canyon Chamber of Commerce, touts the city as "The Gateway to the Grand Canyon."

Old U.S. 66 once intersected the town and Williams, reportedly, was the last town on the old highway to be bypassed. Even though Interstate 40 does bypass the immediate city, tourists throng at the chamber office seeking information.

Eric Eikenberry, chamber manager, reported there are about 5000 people each month, during the spring and summer, visiting the chamber office, and 2000 to 3000 in the winter months. Eikenberry added that about 56 percent of Williams business is directly related to tourism.

Population in 1985 hovered around 2400 in the city limits but tourists swell that figure. Arizona motorists know that Williams is a hub of several lakes, such as Cataract, Dogtown, Kaibab, White Horse. Fishing, hiking, colorful drives including that to Sycamore Canyon and skiing are attractions.

Williams pays homage to mountain man Bill Williams

An eight-mile drive through the towering pines and quaking aspens to Dogtown Lake proved a good summer choice. A cool breeze jostled the pines during a picnic lunch with frolicking squirrels and a blue jay providing unexpected entertainment. Two senior citizens shared the relaxing interlude before picking up fishing gear and lawn chairs and heading for the lake side.

The Grand Canyon Deer Farm, eight miles east of Williams, offers a different experience and attracts a share of visitors.

Back in downtown Williams, tourists browsed about and a busload of Japanese reveled in an Indian artifacts store. It is interesting that a section of the town has been declared an historic business area under provisions of the National Historic Preservation Act.

There is a variety of motels from which to choose. One choice was the Mountain Side Inn, where the room was spacious and beds good. On a June night, the chilly temperature prompted visitors to reach for blankets.

The many restaurants cater to a variety of tastes and pocketbooks. Dinner at Rod's Steak House, a veteran restaurant, was excellent. Diners studied the miniature menus in the shape of a steer and backed by a well known poem: "I like to live in a little town, where trees meet over the street; Where you wave your hand and say 'hello' to everyone you meet . . ."

The verse seems appropriate for this town founded in 1880 and still host to the thousands who sample its hospitality and sylvan setting.

Dogtown Lake, one of several in the Williams area

Ashfork street scene along old 66

ASH FORK
with the "way out West" look

The Harvey Girls no longer claim top interest at the Escalante Hotel, nor does old Highway 66 throb with heavy cross-country traffic as it meanders through town.

In fact, the Santa Fe Harvey House long since was leveled and Interstate 40 circumvents the heart of the town, heading on to Kingman and California or points east.

Gone are the bustling days when Ash Fork was a rail center for cattle shipping and excitement reigned over the Peavine rail line to Prescott and ultimately to Phoenix.

All that is part of the celebrated past of Ash Fork, which observed its centennial in June 1982.

A Santa Fe line branches from Williams with freight through Ash Fork enroute to Prescott and Phoenix. The depot with its "Ash Fork" sign stands idle. The old clock, its time once checked daily with headquarters in Topeka, no longer ticks away on the station wall.

There are keepsakes of Ash Fork's souvenir past.

There is the old gray, weather-beaten Methodist Church building, idle and forlorn, on Fifth Street. The White House Hotel edifice stands along Old 66, its lobby chairs in orderly vacancy.

Ash Fork was so named because it was first established at the fork of three riverbeds or arroyos. The original town burned in 1893 and was rebuilt on the opposite side of the tracks. The town suffered a devastating fire in the mid-1970s.

Population of Ash Fork in 1980 was tabbed at 446, but some place the mid-80s decade estimate much higher. Motorists can spend a comfortable night in the small-town atmosphere and eat a good meal. A sign at the Ash Fork Inn noted "Smile. We're open."

Ash Fork's Chamber of Commerce disbanded, reports Bob Glover, one of its former officers.

Glover is known for creating "Personals by Bob,"—attractive desk signs featuring wood-routed names implanted with metal inlay. He gave one to President Reagan, he said.

By 1985, a new truck stop and grocery market had been added, and cross-country trucks still stopped in the town.

"This is a place for light industry," Glover contended. "We do have a trainable labor pool and it is a relatively cheap labor pool."

A sign beside the highway entering town proclaims: "Ash Fork,

Old church building in Ashfork—a reminder of yesteryear

22 ASH FORK (North Central Arizona)

Flagstone quarry near Ashfork bolsters economy

the Flagstone Capital of the USA." Flagstone operations are probably the major business here and there are several sandstone quarries in the Seligman-Ash Fork-Williams area.

In 1984, it was big news when the town gained a bank. The Stockmen's Bank, with its antique decor including an old vault from Chicago, is a bright note in the town.

The town has several churches, elementary and high schools, a volunteer fire department, motels and restaurants. Years ago, water was brought in by rail tanker delivery, but the town now has its own water well. The governing body in 1985 was through the Yavapai Board of Supervisors.

Glover, a resident here 32 years, appraised the town.

"This is not a place to come to sightsee to any great extent," he said, "or to find night-life or gourmet food.

"However, if you can sit back and watch the sunset, listen to a coyote serenade at night and enjoy a little peace and quiet without sirens and pressure—then Ash Fork is a place to come to.

"It isn't for the young and restless," he added.

Ash Fork, at 5,142 ft. elevation, offers scenic vistas. The highest mountains of the Kaibab and Coconino National Forests dominate the eastern horizon.

It's true. The town does have "a way out West" look.

SELIGMAN
on old Route 66

A westbound Santa Fe freight train throbbed on the tracks in front of the old Seligman depot in 1980 and from the west the beacon light of a diesel engine signalled its approach.

Train employees—including a svelte, blonde, young woman—ended and began a shift here on the lap between Winslow and Needles.

Historically, Seligman is a train oriented town. In 1980, it still was the main economic heartbeat of this remote little town along old U.S. Highway 66.

(Times have changed in this town. On February 5, 1985, according to *Arizona Republic* files, Seligman lost its status as a division-crew change point on the railroad's line. Santa Fe officials announced the depot would be closed and local railroad jobs cut as clerical positions would no longer be needed.)

The new highway I-40 slightly bypasses the town, but there are travelers who still swing off the freeway for a night in the town.

Sunset was casting its last pink rays as diners relished a steak dinner ($5.75 for an 8-oz. ribeye) in the Brass Cart Restaurant. Chino Street, once busy with U.S. 66 travel, was all but deserted. Across the street, lights signalled the Black Cat Bar, and a block beyond a neon-lighted cross atop the Catholic Church beamed serenely.

Seligman, elevation 5250 feet, was established in the 1880s when the railroad branch from Prescott to the main line was built. The junction spawned a new town that became known as Prescott Junction. When the Ash Fork branch to Prescott was built, the branch rails to this town were removed. The community continued to exist, but since it was no longer a rail junction, the townspeople sought a new moniker.

According to *Arizona Republic* files, Seligman is named for Jesse Seligman, who once covered the area as a peddler. Later, he was associated with a New York banking firm bearing his name and also connected with the Atlantic-Pacific Railroad.

Before the days of diesel engines, there was a railroad maintenance building here. The Fred Harvey house was closed in the 1950s.

An oldtimer recalled that the 1920s were good cattle years and the dozens of cowboys who converged on the town Saturday nights raised "plenty of hell."

Santa Fe locomotive is "on track" at Seligman

An overnight stay gives a cursory view of the place. Our visit had topped a backwoods approach to Seligman, via the Williamson Valley-Simmons road and a lunch sashay detour at Walnut Creek. The gravel road with dips was good but dusty.

Accommodations at one motel (there were several) was $19.97 for two. The owner enlivened our introduction to the town stating facetiously the place could be seen in a two-minute tour. He did, however, extol the clean air.

On Railroad Avenue, there were old, vacant houses. Elsewhere, most houses were vintage, one boasting an antler decorated front fence.

There was a small grocery store, garages, bars. At the Thunderbird Indian Store, owner Catherine Wilder, a former trader at Peach Springs, displayed good artifacts.

Homer Davis, the rock shop owner, said he could tell people much about rocks if they hung around long enough.

There was little to do at night except retire to the motel and black and white television.

Major item on the agenda next day was a visit at the Grand Canyon Caverns, an interesting attraction 22 miles west, off Route 66.

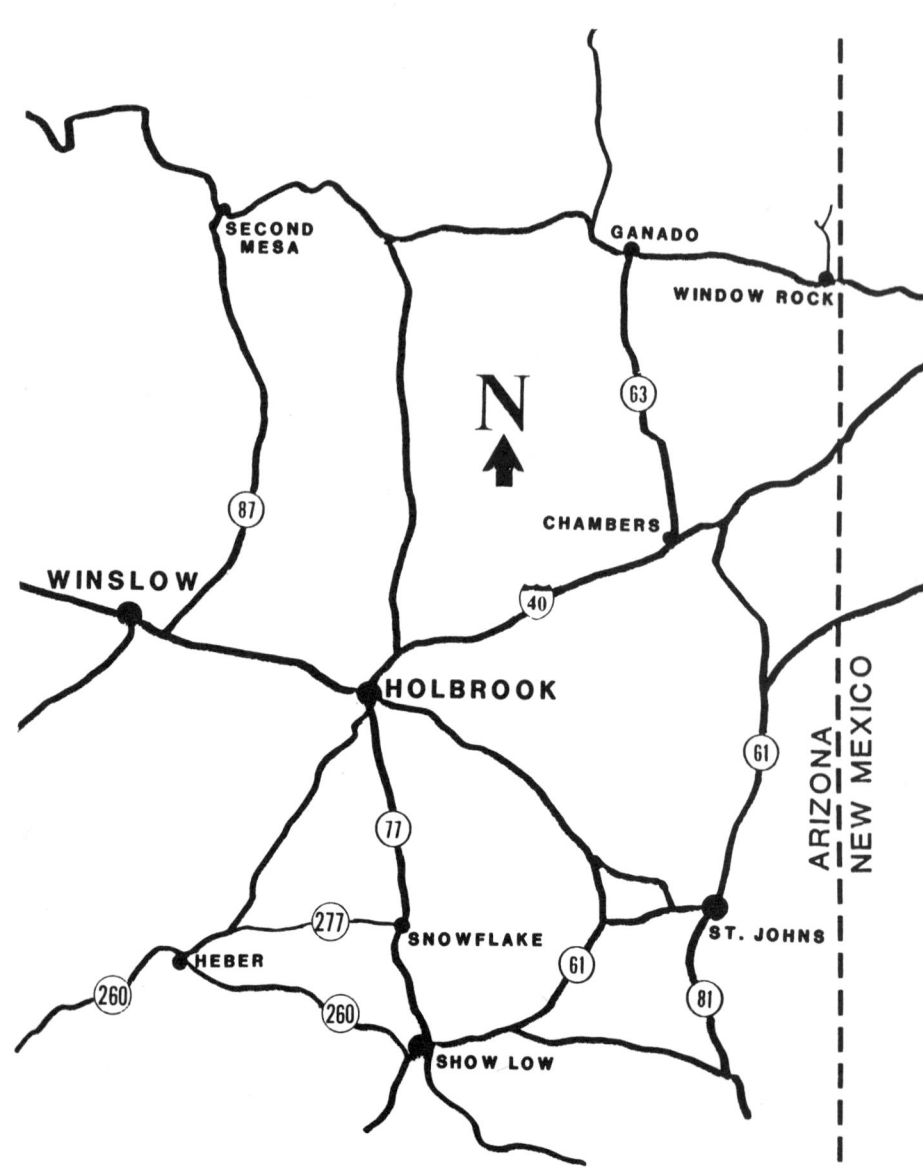

NORTHEAST

SECOND MESA
high in Hopi land

The Hopi Cultural Center, perched on a windswept mesa in Hopi Land, offers a unique travel experience and opportunity to spend a night among the Hopis—"the people of peace."

A night or two here provides a good introduction into the quiet culture of the Hopis, traditionally an agricultural people. Not to be overlooked, by any means, is the chance to taste traditional Hopi food.

Center menus and brochures refer to the area as "at the center of the universe." Perhaps it is, from a Hopi viewpoint.

The high mesas of Hopi country—the First, Second and Third Mesas—scene several Indian villages. Old Oraibi, a few miles away, is one of the oldest continuously inhabited settlements in the United States. To see the place with its ancient houses clutching to a mesa is to look at antiquity.

The Hopi Cultural Center that includes a 33-unit motel and restaurant also has gift shops and a small museum. Shops in the center and elsewhere in the area feature Indian artifacts—pottery, kachina dolls, jewelry, textiles and paintings. To help acquaint visitors with the area, guided tours for a fee are available through the center.

The cultural center, owned by the tribe and leased to private enterprise, is on State 264 between Tuba City and Keams Canyon. For variety, the return trip can be made via State 87 to Winslow.

At a dinner on a crisp cool April, the restaurant featured a pleasant mix of Hopis and visitors. The restaurant, its front windows offering a distant vista of San Francisco Peaks, has been enlarged to accommodate 250 persons.

While the menu at the Hopi Center offers a variety of conventional entrees—steaks, seafood and chicken—Hopi food is the novelty. Savory entrees bearing Hopi names include one of pink beans, ground beef and red chili, and another of Hopi corn and lamb with baked green chili. Both entrees are served with Indian fry bread and honey. Another guest termed the Hopi taco delicious. Hopi breakfast features include pancakes of blue cornmeal.

Visitors in Hopi villages and fascinating scenery should remember they are amid a different culture and obey restrictions including stringent bans on photography. Visitors may check at the center

Hopi Cultural Center at Second Mesa

about restrictions. Hopis are governed by tribal council in headquarters near Old Oraibi.

A must in Second Mesa is a visit to the Hopi Arts and Crafts Silvercraft Cooperative building near the cultural center. Guild craftsmen may be seen at work and there is an extensive array of Indian jewelry and large gallery.

Hopis encountered were friendly, helpful.

Memories of the quiet night and the general serenity of a night with the Hopis linger on. And on.

WINDOW ROCK
scenic wonder in Navajo land

The late sun bathed the "haystacks," great sandstone monoliths, in added orange splashes.

Outside the Window Rock Motor Inn restaurant, marigolds and petunias danced in decorative tubsful in the wind.

Inside, Navajo waitresses—their squaw dress skirts and turquoise jackla earrings swishing—deftly served patrons.

Piped music beamed from a Gallup, New Mexico station in modern beat. A clock on the wall told Navajo time, an hour later in the summer than Arizona time.

Travelers were not only in Navajo Land but in the capital of the Navajo Nation. It was a taste of a different culture. The vibes were different, pleasant.

This remote town, a half-mile or so from the New Mexico border boasts one of the most photographed natural phenomenons of the southwest. It is the Tsegahozani, "The Rock with a Hole in It," listed as one of the seven wonders of the Navajo world.

The distinguishing trademark and namesake of the community, Window Rock in Apache County, is a great window, carved through centuries by the wind, sand and water. It towers in red sandstone 47 feet in average diameter and 100 feet above the picnic area near its base.

The maze of government administration buildings huddled in the Navajo capital are mostly in complementary shades of the sandstone hills. Among them is the octagonal shape Navajo Nation Council Building. A bell at the entrance, given to the tribe by the Santa Fe Railway, has called councilmen to session.

Window Rock, a novel locale, is reached by turning off I-40 at Lupton and heading north on paved but rough Indian Route 12. The 26-mile drive passes colorful hills, forest and valley areas. Houses and hogans with bright hued roofs add to the panorama.

The Navajo Museum housed with Navajo Arts and Crafts Enterprises, a subsidiary of the Navajo Nation, in Window Rock gives extra insight into the Indian Land.

There was no charge for the museum, open Mondays through Fridays, but contributions may be made. On the register book, one visitor commented: "Isaiah 26:3."

The two-story Window Rock Motor Inn, owned by the tribe offers 56 spacious rooms. Menu special for the day (a 1983 visit) at the restaurant, was meatloaf, $5.50. Mutton stew with fried bread

Famed Window Rock at Navajo Nation capital—one of seven wonders of Navajo world

was $3. No liquor, of course, is sold.

The famed window at Window Rock is fenced off—for good reason. A few years ago, according to a Navajo publication, part of the "ceiling" of the window broke off and fell crashing to the earth below.

Since then, climbing the rock is forbidden. The scenic wonder "must be viewed at a respectful distance." The sandstone, of which many scenic wonders of the Navajo reservation are composed, is susceptible to deterioration, the Navajos note.

Window Rock, the natural wonder, is a sacred place to the Navajos.

A sidetrip to Fort Defiance, some six miles north of Window

Rock, is locale of the Window Rock High School, a hospital and streets where old shade arches overhead.

The old Fort Defiance military post was established in 1851, but the last of the buildings have been razed. The fort, established in defiance of the Navajos and so named, involves considerable history. A final treaty was signed with the Navajos in 1868.

The village contains several churches, including the Episcopal Good Shepherd Mission, some parts dating from 1904. Tall cupola of today's church with its turquoise color shutters may be seen from a distance.

One of the interesting sights is the Navajo Veteran's Cemetery on a hill, where a U.S. flag, large or small, fluttered in the wind from most graves. Focal point, too, is a 155 mm howitzer cannon that was presented in 1963 by the U.S. Marine Corps "in honor of the Navajo Indian tribe."

The Navajo Code Talkers of WWII will long be remembered for the role they played in using their tribal language as a code to transmit military messages which the enemy could not decipher.

Window Rock is the scene of the Navajo National Zoological Park, featuring birds and animals of the reservation.

St. Michael's Mission is a showplace in the Window Rock area and nearby is St. Michael's Historical Museum, a quaint building that invites inspection. The building is billed as the first St.

Navajo Nation council chambers nestled near sandstone hill at Window Rock

St. Michaels Historical Museum, in 1898 building, is listed in National Register of Historic Places

Franciscan Mission on the Navajo Reservation and was the forerunner of the present large mission complex.

Constructed in 1898, it was restored to its original condition as an official Bicentennial project, and is now listed on the National Register of Historical Places.

The museum exhibits the Crucifixion rug, woven by Asdza Yazzie, wife of the first tribal chairman, Chee Dodge in 1936.

The museum was open daily from Memorial Day through Labor Day and the remainder of the year by appointment.

The St. Michael School, about a mile away, opened in December 1902. Modern high school buildings were completed in 1950.

History, a different culture and spectacular scenery do combine in a unique package in this far recess of Arizona.

Navajo Veterans' Cemetery from vantage point near howitzer cannon at Ft. Defiance

CHAMBERS
near the Petrified Forest

This faraway spot, Chambers, five miles south of the Navajo Reservation, scarcely can be called a town.

It is a place with a past, located along busy I-40. Some number the population between 80 and 100.

Yet, despite its tiny size, Chambers boasts a motel and restaurant that operate in a style belying the remoteness. It's all packaged in the 52-unit Chieftain Motel.

The settlement, in barren, far-west appeal country cut through by the Puerco River, has claimed a post office since 1907.

Carolyn Jones, postmaster since 1979, is a native of Chambers, born on her father's homestead.

"I haven't lived any place else," the mother of five said. "I like living in Chambers. It's home."

Jones said the post office carries 244 postal boxes and 35 general delivery patrons. Bulk of patrons are Navajos, but tourists at the motel often mail scenic postcards.

Besides the motel and restaurant, there are the Chambers' Trading Post, service station, the E-Z Market, a few scattered homes.

A cluster of trailers, buildings and old cottonwood trees along

Amtrak train speeds through Chambers

"Newspaper Rock" in Petrified Forest

the Santa Fe railroad mark the site of Chambers' earlier days. A railroad sign "Chambers" and huge black water storage tank, flank the place where Amtrak trains speed through at around 85 mph twice a day. Freight cars with trailing cabooses also ply the rails.

A night in 1983, in a modern room at The Chieftain was $35.02 for two. Big influx of on-the-road travelers is in the summertime.

Dinner at The Chieftain restaurant was in colorful, well-appointed surroundings—chandeliers with red lights, red upholstered booths and steer horns for extra wall decor.

Since Chambers is close to the reservation, we chose the Navajo taco dinner made with Indian fry bread—cost, $4.75. The pork chop dinner, billed as "high off the hog," was $5.95.

Travelers who like to browse will appreciate the well-stocked gift shop. Historians say Charles Chambers ran a trading post here for years before the railroad came in 1881.

According to *Arizona Place Names,* the name was changed for a time to Halloysite, after bentonite clay which was mined four miles northeast. In June 1930, the name again became Chambers.

While in the area, travelers may want to include a visit to the Petrified Forest National Monument. Turnoff to the monument is 22 miles west on Interstate-40. The 27-mile scenic tour through the monument takes travelers into wild rugged country splashed with riotous colors and mountains in fanciful shapes.

In the mid-1800s, U.S. Army mappers and surveyors came into the area and carried back East stories of a remarkable "Painted Desert with its trees turned to stone."

After a period of using the wood for souvenirs and various commercial projects, action was taken to protect the petrified wood. In 1906, select "forests" were set aside as a national monument. The monument has since been enlarged and today the Painted Desert is included.

An entire day can be spent in the monument. In the Rainbow Forest, a "Great Logs Walk," a half-mile trail, wends through the park's petrified logs.

A side junket within the monument leads to "Newspaper Rock." Some sightseers decide not to make the 120 steps leading down to the rock. The clear petroglyphs, however, were worth the exertion to this visitor.

A marker explains "While aboriginal Americans were making these petroglyphs, Marco Polo was on an epic journey to Asia."

Petrified Forest National Park is a nearby attraction to Chambers

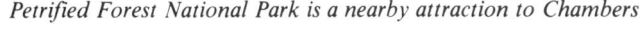

ST. JOHNS
You'll stay longer, too!

Few small Arizona towns can top the scenario here in remoteness, friendliness, history and proximity to scenic points of interest.

The composite personality is inviting. In fact, we planned to spend a July night and day here but stayed a second night.

There was a special bonus. We couldn't help but share the pervading excitement as the town celebrated the annual Pioneer Days.

At the Apache County Historical Museum, the pride and joy of the county, a worker added touches to a parade float. The museum is a "must see" place.

There was a pioneer celebration campfire that night where oldtimers and friends cooked meals and reminisced. The Circle K Market was a beehive of coming and going. A city patrolman swinging his car in the lot and pausing to talk to outsiders, placed the town's population near 4500.

Nearby, an outdoor dance band struck up foot-tapping music outdoors. Pedestrians and shopkeepers were friendly. The July night was cool at the elevation of 5725 feet.

Don't expect posh motels and restaurants. A dinner at JR's Steakhouse (a small top sirloin, $6.95) was tasty and so was breakfast at the Coach Lantern Restaurant. Our king-size bed and room ($31 plus tax), in 1982, at the Sky Riders Motel was comfy.

The next morning, the interesting pioneer parade with a maze of floats took more than an hour to pass in review.

Historically, according to information gleaned at the museum, St. Johns was first settled by ox-train drivers of Solomon Barth, who contracted to supply hay and grain to Fort Apache military forces.

In 1971, the Barths settled a group of drivers and families here. According to one version, the settlers chose the town name of "San Juan" after Dona Maria de San Juan Baca, who with her husband settled on the "Coloradito" at El Vado (the ford). Postal authorities ordered the name changed to St. Johns, the English version of San Juan.

From the Phoenix area, St. Johns can be reached via Payson, the Mogollon Rim and beautiful Apache Sitgreaves Forest. Out of Show Low and headed for Concho, motorists must approach the intersection of U.S. Highway 60 and State 61 carefully.

Along St. Johns' main street

St. Johns, incidentally, is the county seat of Apache County, the seventh of Arizona's 15 counties to be created. Some describe the town as "a sleepy hollow" of some 1500 people until the Salt River Project began building the nearby Coronado Generating Plant in 1975. That touched off growth in population, homes and businesses. The plant reportedly has a permanent payroll of several hundred.

Lyman's Lake State Park is about 12 miles south of the town along U.S. Highway 180. The 1500-acre lake is fed by snowmelt from the slopes of Mounts Baldy and Escudilla, 30 miles to the south. The lake was formed in 1912 by damming the Little Colorado River to form an irrigation reservoir and the water level fluctuates seasonally.

The several park facilities include a boat launching ramp, and the state parks office reported large mouth bass, walleye, northern pike, channel and blue catfish the predominate catch.

Back in St. Johns, the Apache County Court House, with its 1917 cornerstone, is wreathed in old grandeur. And, chances are that visitors will long remember the chimes that peal—ever so melodiously—from St. Johns Catholic Church.

SNOWFLAKE
"Home of the Pioneers"

A sign at the gateway to this town, founded in 1878, greets: "Welcome to Snowflake. Home of the Pioneers."

History is big in this remote town located 27 miles south of Holbrook at the intersection of State 277 and 77 in Navajo County.

Probably the biggest eye-catcher to newcomers is the array of venerably old houses, some of two-story gable designs in brick or frame.

Taking the cake must be the three-story James M. Flake house with gingerbread trim. Most novel feature is the white picket fence that adds an ornate touch to the rooftop deck. The house, built in 1895, is now on the National Register of Historic Places.

Chock full of history, too, is the Jesse Nathaniel Smith brick home fronted with picket fence. It is designated as a "Pioneer

James M. Flake house, built in 1895, is another historic Snowflake residence

Memorial Home."

A marker in the front yard proclaims Smith (1834-1906) "a pioneer, colonizer, church leader and family man" and a first cousin of Mormon Prophet Joseph Smith.

The message also tells of his "five loving and devoted wives" who bore him 44 "worthy children."

Even the town hall occupies a slice of history. An outside sign reads, "Old School House Built in 1891." The building is modernized to function as town hall, council chambers, police station and library.

Historians say the community and surrounding farmland are on land settled in 1873 by James Stinson. Snowflake was founded in 1878 and is named for two Mormon pioneers, Erastus Snow and William J. Flake.

Sanford Flake, in 1983 police chief for 22 years, is a great grandson of William Flake. His father, S. Eugene Flake, was born in the historic Flake house.

Another old house in Snowflake, appropriately, has been converted into the Silver Creek Senior Citizens' Center.

Town Librarian Jerri Reidhead said the library contains 36,500 books. She quickly can produce books dealing with Snowflake

(Northeast Arizona) SNOWFLAKE 39

history.

Snowflake, some 24 miles north of the colorful Mogollon Rim country, was incorporated with a common council in 1948.

Today, Main Street is broad and flanked with trees and alongside Pioneer Park.

Shopping was brisk at the Pioneer Market, and Pioneer Ceramics, ensconced in an old house on Main Street, was a hub of activity. At "Something Else," an antique cup, lavishly decorated, tempted purchase.

One of the area's leading industries is the Southwest Forest Industries paper mill, on a 640-acre site 15 miles west of Snowflake. Pig farms are also important in the economy.

A night at the Cedar Motel, billed as a "Best Restin' Motel," found clean spacious facilities at $27.30 for two.

Dinner at the Long Horn Steak House was excellent, featuring sirloin steak (women's size), a salad bar and delicious broccoli soup, at an $8.25 dinner price.

Dining room decor was enhanced by a gallery of oil paintings by Chief Flake, restaurant co-owner. At lunchtime, The Grub Stake filled the bill with homemade vegetable soup. Coffee was 10¢ a cup.

While Snowflake was about 65 percent of Mormon faith, the community now reflects different cultures and religion. There are modern style homes along with the old.

A huge "S" on a mountain ridge near the town reflects community pride and interest. Its white coat is maintained each year by Snowflake High School freshmen.

Snowflake is a pleasant place to visit.

Historic Jesse Nathaniel Smith home welcomes visitors in Snowflake

HEBER
cool retreat on the Rim!

A quiet restful community along State 260 in Navajo County, Heber is couched in a lush valley and, meandering through, are Black Canyon Creek and Buckskin Wash.

An old town, founded in 1883, Heber in early April 1983, was in midst of plans for its centennial observance in July.

Cliff Johnson, C of C president, and member Kelly Clark were appraising the first batch of commemorative caps emblazoned "1883—Heber, Arizona, Centennial—1983." The celebration promised to be a colorful occasion.

Arizona Place Names notes that Heber stems from a Mormon migration to Arizona in 1876 and 1877. The place derives its name from Heber C. Kimball, a prominent member of the church.

The spacious LDS Church was built in the early 1960s at a cost of $230,000 (according to ***Arizona Republic*** files), after a fire destroyed an earlier church.

It is difficult for an outsider to see where Heber ends and Overgaard begins. The combined population of the two communities was estimated at 2500 to 3000. The cool summer clime and the number of summer homes swell the seasonal population.

Johnson said the community was experiencing growth because of its attraction to retirees. A principal economic factor in Heber was the Evergreen sawmill. The ***Pine Graphics Shopper,*** a weekly paper stemming from nearby Overgaard, informs the community of grassroots news.

Heber, at 6439 ft., offered at least two motels and one restaurant in 1983.

Summer months find Black Canyon Lake a drawing card for visitors.

It was spring by the calendar, but winter by the weather and barely spitting snow when visitors left Heber with Black Canyon Lake the scenic target. Checking first at the Forest Service Ranger Station in Overgaard, travelers were given a map of the forest area.

Forest Road 86 exited Heber for the 13-mile trek to the lake. Pine cones were bunched along the gravel road in the pine-scented forest and sunshine flitted in and out among the clouds. A bushy-tailed squirrel dashed across the road, while a thick blanket of snow silhouetted the pines.

A sign at a fork in the road noted Black Canyon Lake four miles away. Later, aspens in clusters looked stark and naked amid the snow. Stopping the car to breathe in the beauty, travelers found the silence absolute in the deep forest.

The sun peeked out a moment as Black Canyon Lake, fringed with pines, shimmered in jewel-like beauty ahead. Not a fisherman was in sight.

Back in Heber, rooms at the Canyon View Motel, touted as "Sleep Cheap in the Cool Pines," were spacious and comfortable.

Dinner at Zane's Steak House in neighboring Overgaard was a highlight and breakfast at the Rim Restaurant in Heber was also good.

For sure, Heber would offer a cool retreat in summertime.

Light snow encircles Black Canyon Lake

EAST

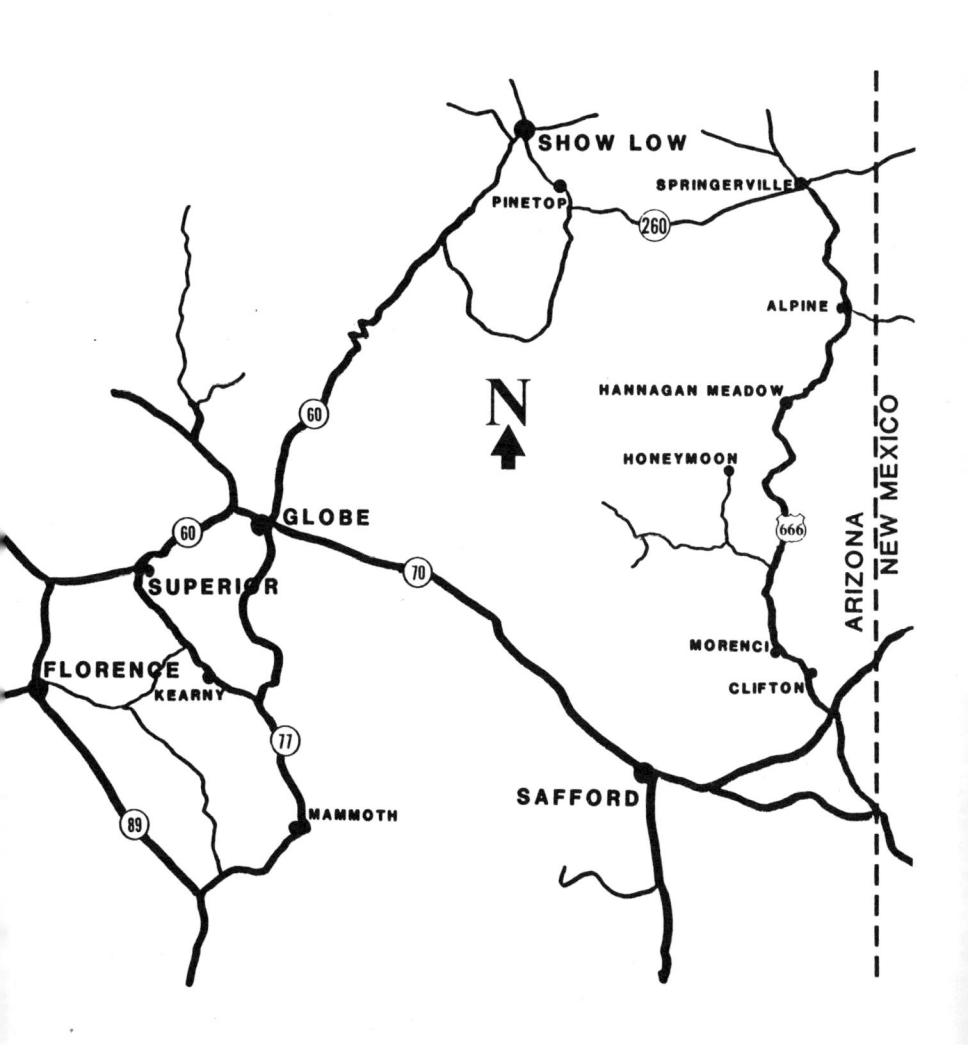

Map of Eastern Arizona 43

ALPINE
scenery rivaling the Alps!

This community got its name, some say, after travelers from Switzerland visited here and declared the scenery rivaled that of the Alps.

Indeed, Alpine's greatest attraction for the casual visitor must be its rustic beauty, and a night there can provide a relaxing interlude.

Alpine, a short distance from the New Mexico state line, is located at the junction of U.S. 180 and U.S. 666, the famed Coronado Trail. Coronado is said to have explored the region in 1540 while searching for the "Seven Cities of Cibola."

Historians note that Alpine developed from a log-house "fort," comprised of a number of small low-roofed cabins joined in a circle with portholes for the settlers to shoot through—in case of Indians. Oldtimers recall that the fort was never attacked by Indians because of the appearance of strength it gave. The fort-buildings, just below the present Alpine, were torn down in 1884.

In time, Mormon settlers moved in to buy out the claims of the pioneering Anderson Bush and others. According to files of the *Arizona Republic,* leader of the Mormon settlers was Fred Hamblin, brother of the famed scout and missionary Jacob Hamblin, who lived here in his later years.

A Fort Bush Monument, erected in honor of Alpine pioneers who sought safety here, was dedicated in June 1953.

Several restaurants mark today's Alpine, and the Apache Sitgreaves National Forest Ranger Station is on U.S. 666 in the community. Along the main street, the two-story Clarence Jepsen house with a mellowed patina wrought by 80 years is a standout.

A pleasant evening meal at reasonable prices was available in a 1981 visit at the M and J Corral Restaurant. Top sirloin dinners were $9.95; a trout meal, $6.95; and chicken-fried steak, $4.95. Customers pronounced the homemade fruit pies delicious.

Alpine is a small village and it doesn't take long to see the place, even browsing a bit at the general store along the main street. Townspeople placed the population at 500 in the winter and 1200 in the summer, including summertime residents.

A night for two at the Mountain Hi Lodge, modern with black and white television, was $18.34.

At 8,030 ft. altitude, the mountain town spells a night of cool sleeping, even in mid-July.

Perhaps the greatest stanza in the Arizona fall foliage song of the forest occurs in the Alpine area, along a lap of the famed Coronado Trail. Luna Lake, some three miles east of Alpine, is a summer attraction.

Apache Sitgreaves National Forest ranger station at Alpine

HANNAGAN MEADOW
in a rustic forest setting

Christmas lights sparkled along the eaves of the Hannagan Meadow Lodge in a late May sojourn.

Elsewhere, smoke spiraled from a cabin where inside the woodburning stove radiated comforting warmth.

The 9100 ft. altitude made the toasty warmth welcome, and towering forest trees added a spicy aroma. Fronting the lodge is a large meadow where deer sometimes appear to the delight of visitors.

On a May night, the temperature dipped to 36 degrees, while patches of old snow occasionally embellished the forest scene. Coyotes added their own notes to the novelty of a night in the forest. Other animals, even bears, sometimes wander into the setting.

Introducing the change of pace is the beauty of the Coronado Trail (U.S. 666) enroute from Clifton to Hannagan Meadow.

A highway marker beyond Morenci noted that animals might be seen the next 50 miles. Sure enough, three young elk gamboled in a wooded area.

The Coronado Trail requires close attention by the driver, as the road twists and turns in spiraling heights and descents. In one area, narrow bridges were encountered and on a sharp curve the posted speed was 10 mph. The Mogollon Rim country where quaking aspens intersperse spruce and pine provides eye-catching scenes.

Hannagan Meadow Lodge, reportedly, is one of the oldest in the state, the original construction completed in 1926.

It is interesting to note that *Arizona Place Names* states the place was named for Robert Hannagan (note the spelling) who ran cattle in the meadow in early days. However, the spelling is "Hannagan" on the Arizona state map.

The lodge dining room, with large fireplace, overlooks the meadow. There is also a store and bar.

Some guests stay in the lodge, others in the cabins with fireplace or woodburning stove. The cabins are rustic, bed linens are furnished. The cabin brochure asks guests to bring towels. There are no room phones, television or radio. During the winter, it is suggested guests bring electric blankets. There is a summer trailer park.

Hannagan Meadow Lodge—a quiet retreat at 9100 feet

The lodge is 23 miles south of Alpine and 266 miles from Phoenix.

During the winter, lodge owners recommend travelers go through Alpine to get to the lodge. When Highway 666 is closed due to snow, the road between Alpine and Hannagan is normally passable but the road south from Hannagan to Clifton is unpassable, according to lodge information.

In the wintertime, the lodge area offers cross-country skiing. Summertime, there is fishing, and in the fall, hunting. Reservations are advisable and current information may be obtained by calling the lodge or writing, Box 335, Alpine, AZ 85920.

Along the (rugged)
HONEYMOON trail!

Travelers with a yen for backwoods and off-the-beaten path travel may find Honeymoon the rugged answer.

You don't believe there is a place in Arizona called Honeymoon? Surprise!

Look at the Arizona state map and note the tiny square designation inside the west border of Greenlee County. Yes, it is remote!

A call to the U.S. Ranger station earlier in Clifton revealed the trail to Honeymoon could be navigated. The signal was clear (at the time anyway). Eagle Creek, however, must be crossed.

There are tables and pit toilets at the Honeymoon picnic area but no potable water. The ranger wished the caller a good trip.

Armed with an Apache-Sitgreaves National Forest map ($1 at the ranger station) and topographic maps of the trail area, we were on our way. Our Jeep Wagoneer also carried ample water, gasoline, picnic supplies and civilian band radio.

Traditionally, it seems, Honeymoon is so-called because a forest ranger years ago brought his bride to an area cabin that, reportedly, now is privately owned.

The mileage was carefully checked at the turn off U.S. 666 (The Coronado Trail) on to the Upper Eagle Creek Road. The sign read "Eagle Creek, 15 miles," and "Honeymoon, 22." The gravel road was well marked along the way but rough in places and, as could be expected, dusty.

Driver and I kept a mileage log that is basically correct even though it wound up a mile short. The log is, at least, a guideline.

MILE 1.9 - Note a sign "Firewood Area." The road meanders through the cactus-and-cedar-dotted terrain with canyon on one side.

MILE 3.7 - A mailbox proclaimed N O Bar Ranch and to the left was a small corral.

MILE 4.5 - A small stream trickled across the road. Lavender flowered bushes were in bloom in late May.

MILE 5 - A washed-out bridge, trail narrowed to one car width and close by a stream again trickled across the road.

MILE 5.3 - Sheep Wash Road turnoff. Stay on Forest Road 217. Soon a sign, "Narrow Steep Rd."

48 HONEYMOON (Eastern Arizona)

MILE 5.7 - We stopped to photograph brilliant orange flowers. Sorry, my book on wildflowers was at home. I like to identify flowers and sometimes am leery of wildflowers—not knowing which may be poisonous.

MILE 8.9 - A sign said "Big Dry," but there was water in the wash.

MILE 9.1 - Mailboxes and a ranch. In the next few minutes, four pickup trucks passed. There are several ranches along the way. Road gets rougher.

MILE 10.4 - Sign said "Bear Canyon."

MILE 11.3 - A windmill, and ahead a road sign, "Eagle Creek, 3 miles, Honeymoon, 10." A little beyond, a marker "Eagle Recreation Trail." Stay on 217. Not far away, another sign intrigued, "Eagle Creek School." For two cents, we would have gone to see the school. A black crow flew over.

MILE 13.8 - A neat sign: "Ford," and beyond the marker, "Eagle Creek." Our Wagoneer easily plowed across without resorting to four-wheel drive. Incidentally, not once on our May junket was four-wheel drive necessary. Don't travel the road in inclement weather.

Yes, there is a place called Honeymoon in Arizona

The sign "ford" signals Eagle Creek ahead on road to Honeymoon

MILE 16 - Another "Ford" sign with Eagle Creek at hand. The expanse seemed larger. A herd of cattle scurried on the sideline. Timber is taller, giant cottonwood trees arched over the trail. Soon, a sign, "Private Land next mile."

MILE 18.5 - Another creek, presumably Eagle. This time Driver noted car brakes afterwards were wet and drove accordingly. Beyond, a road sign indicated "San Carlos Indian Reservation, 1 mile."

MILE 21 - Honeymoon at hand. Time for picnic.

Lunch, in a delightful setting, was at a table beneath a giant spreading ash and sycamore tree with noisy, rustling Eagle Creek a few feet away. Aside from the creek and the birds, there were no other sounds. Nary a human being came by during the lunch repast. As we packed up picnic gear, a pickup truck swished by.

A recognizable former ranger cabin was not found. There was a trailer home beyond the sign "Dead End Road—not maintained for public travel."

Overhead the sky was deep blue but the clouds assembling were not so fleecy. It seemed high time to backtrack from the peaceful forest scene.

The rugged trail, the spring flowers and Eagle Creek had combined for a novel travel sashay along the trail to Honeymoon.

MORENCI
old—and new—mining town!

The open pit copper mine gapes here in gargantuan dimensions, its amphitheater-like sides reflecting changing hues in salmon-pink, rust and gray.

It was the encroachment of mining activities that brought about the demise of some old buildings, including the historic Morenci Hotel and the Morenci Club House.

It was in the mid-1960s that the Phelps Dodge Corp. began construction of the new Morenci, some two miles away. A few old Morenci area homes exist on all area hills.

The transition involved displacement of many, many families. The project took several years to complete, including construction of housing for the families and related facilities.

The company town today includes the Morenci Motel, where visitors can be comfortably accommodated. A spacious room with a queen-size bed contains television beamed from Phoenix. Meals were savory at the motel's Copper Room Restaurant.

The town square contains a large Phelps Dodge Mercantile Store with stock ranging from groceries and furniture to clothing and novelties.

There are several churches, including the eye-catching Holy Cross Catholic Church, a bowling alley, hospital, theater. The town square also involves privately-owned businesses, including the Kopper Kettle Kafe and a jewelry store. The company-owned library provides a quiet retreat and helpful personnel.

Population estimates by residents varied. A Phelps Dodge employee said the company employs about 2000 but not all live here. Two lawmen estimated the population at 3500.

Along the way, the community encountered the vagaries of mining which include a major strike launched in 1983. Mining

Phelps Dodge offices in Morenci

Hotel Morenci, vintage 1890, no longer exists

operations are in progress, however.

It was in 1937 that Phelps Dodge, long entrenched in the old mining community, began the required moving of waste capping for the open pit mine operations.

Arizona Place Names states that by 1955, 570 million tons had been removed, leaving the uppermost level at 5000 feet and the lowest level at 4400 feet.

In 1968, a sign at the open pit noted that development of the low-grade ore body in the pit began in 1937. The first ore was delivered to the newly completed Morenci Reduction Works in 1942. Through 1966, a total of a billion tons of material had been removed, of which 694 million tons were waste rock.

A current visit to the canopied overview area of the vast pit found a train bustling in the deep pit with trucks appearing as toys in the depth below. Areas of the pit may be seen by motorists continuing on U.S. 666 north.

In a typical small town scene, an early morning breakfast at the Kopper Kettle Kafe found patrons enjoying eggs and bacon and the day's first cups of coffee.

Morenci, at 4710 feet altitude, is along the Coronado Trail, U.S. Highway 666, with Clifton its close neighbor.

To spend a night in the company town with its friendly people is to chalk up a different—and pleasant—travel experience.

House with "gingerbread" trim in Clifton

CLIFTON
charismatic old mining town!

As is customary, the fire siren sounds boldly at noon each Wednesday, reverberating against the red cliffs flanking remote Clifton.

In a way, the siren sets the staunch tone which marks this old mining town, the county seat for Greenlee in eastern Arizona. History, gaunt old store facades along Chase Creek Street and the lore and vagaries of mining forge a unique community package.

Its very geography sets the place apart. Clifton is situated between towering canyon walls with an arroyo cut by the meandering San Francisco River.

For newcomers, historic Chase Creek business street is an eye-catching sight, one where imagination can easily take flight. Many buildings are empty, eroding with age. Some flaunt balconies with wrought iron grill balustrades, scroll work and ornate facades with vintage dates.

Elsewhere, visitors can exclaim over the original 1878 jail, crammed into a rock cliff along the main highway. Blasted from "living rock," the plaque says, the jail confined many of the bad men who crowded into the district during its boom days. One story says the builder celebrated so much when the jail was completed that he became the first person therein incarcerated.

The Copper Head Coronado Railroad's first steam locomotive is enshrined nearby. And, in another setting, the 1911 vintage county court house boasts a modern annex.

The town suffered a devastating flood of the San Francisco River in 1906, and there have been other floods in Clifton over the years.

(Carlos Rivera, town manager in 1986, said the Army Corps of Engineers has developed a plan to relocate a portion of Clifton to a mesa area safe from flooding. The process, if authorized and funded through the U.S. Congress, could possibly take three to four years to materialize, he said. Other plans, Rivera said, are to

Souvenir of the past—Copper Head Coronado Railroad locomotive and jailhouse

build a levee along the San Francisco River to protect a remaining portion of the town.)

As part of its history, Clifton weathered a shut down of some mining activity and a lengthy strike at the Phelps Dodge mine. Mining, however, is still the dominate economic factor here. Plans are under consideration to revitalize the historic Chase Creek section.

Evidence of early mining operations may be seen in the area aside from the gigantic open pit and reduction works of Phelps Dodge in neighboring Morenci, some four miles away.

Clifton, at 3,464 ft. elevation and incorporated in 1909, is often referred to as the gateway to the famed Coronado Trail along U.S. 666 between this town and Alpine.

During an overnight visit in Clifton, spacious accommodations were found at the Rode Inn Motel. Dining at the Morenci Motel's Copper Room Restaurant featured a roast beef dinner with a trip to the salad bar.

Al Fernandez, at 84, has lived here since 1914. His memories of the old days are keen, and especially he remembers Chase Creek Street during its heyday.

"It (Clifton) was like the rest of the mining camps. There was a lot of activity," he said. "People didn't have cars like they do now. They would congregate on Chase Creek, go to the pool halls, gambling places, stores."

And, yes, there were the bars and bawdy houses, he said.

The mines were at Metcalf (about seven miles up the road) and in Morenci. The smelter for the Arizona Copper Co., the main employer, later purchased by Phelps Dodge, was in Clifton. There were also the Detroit and Shannon Copper companies. In an earlier period of inactivity, he said, the mine operations shut down in the 1930s. Copper dropped to about four cents a pound.

When Phelps Dodge later gained control, Fernandez said, underground mining was abandoned and open pit mining adopted.

Many buildings on Chase Creek Street were destroyed by fire at the end of 1911 (or early 1912). Some buildings escaped the fire, such as the 1907 dated facade building, once the English Chop House, a Chinese restaurant.

Fernandez, mayor of Clifton in 1958, served many years on the Greenlee County Historical Society Museum board. That building was flooded in a 1983 river rampage, and plans are to develop a museum elsewhere.

County Court House—1911 vintage

CLIFTON (Eastern Arizona)

SUPERIOR
—the Arboretum and "Apache tears"

Rounding a bend on a spiraling strip on U.S. 60 in the Tonto National Forest, this old mining town suddenly looms on the horizon in a splashing spread of buildings.

The small smokestack, guarding the area like a sentinel, no longer belches smoke. And, for that matter, in 1982, the Magma Copper Mine had shut down production here.

The town nestles at 2820 feet, almost surrounded by such imposing mountains as Picket Post, Apache Leap and Iron Mountain.

Downtown, a rose-hued statue, chiseled from native rock and weighing 10 tons, captures the fancy at the intersection of Pinal and Main. It was created by Tommy Macias, a Superior sanitation worker.

Titled "Brotherhood," the statue is sometimes referred to as "Helping Hand" as it shows two men helping each other climb a mountain. The statue was unveiled in October 1982 in ceremonies marking the centennial of this now incorporated town.

Local history notes that Superior was first called Hastings, but later named after an area mine—the Lake Superior and Arizona. The Magma company was established here in 1910.

Town Hall is housed in a former Masonic Temple. The library, in quarters elsewhere, contained some 12,000 books.

Overnight accommodations at the Portal Motel, selected ahead from the phone directory "yellow pages," were not reminiscent of The Hilton. They were, however, comfortable and adequate, and

"Brotherhood" or "Helping Hand" statue was unveiled in downtown Superior during centennial ceremonies

Arboretum draws 70,000 visitors annually

the price tag was a mere $15 a night, plus tax.

Townspeople suggested Los Hermanos as a place to eat. Menu items featured good Mexican food along with other selections.

The town of about 5000 has its own weekly newspaper, the **Superior Sun.**

Superior's claim to a scenic attraction must be the Boyce Thompson Southwestern Arboretum, billed as one of the world's most beautiful and useful gardens. The Arizona State Parks Board and University of Arizona cooperate with the Boyce Thompson Arboretum, Inc., in the living museum.

William Boyce Thompson, a successful mining magnate and philanthropist, decided in the early 1920s to use a portion of his wealth to endow and establish the arboretum.

There is an admission to the arboretum, about three miles west of this town, along U.S. 60. The place includes the Visitor Center and three well-marked scenic trails that invite exploration. More than 70,000 visitors from the U.S. and abroad annually visit the place.

Plan to visit the arboretum in time to lunch in a delightful picnic area with spreading shade trees, tables and benches.

An historical marker along the highway east of the arboretum tells of Picket Post Mountain, a landmark and lookout during

Indian wars and locale for the home of Col. Thompson, arboretum founder. Travelers are tempted to take the next turnoff to Picket Post House, "The Castle on the Rock."

A treat was in store for those who pay the admission fee to see the "castle."

Carolyn Rose, who with her husband, W. Z., then owned the place, conducted a personal tour. The opulence of the furnishings and great natural vistas outside the tall arched windows combined unforgettably.

Rose said the edifice on the hill was built at a cost of $1 million in 1923. Thompson owned mines in Superior, Miami and Clifton, she said. The 26-room home was built as a copy of a monastery Thompson saw in Greece.

The place includes a sizable display of antiques that are for sale.

For a novel experience, visitors in the Superior area in 1982 could visit a place billed as the "Apache Tear Caves." An area was provided where visitors could, for a fee, pick a small pail of "Apache Tears," black obsidian stones with transluscent quality when held to the light.

The tears can be polished and used in jewelry. The stones, according to legend, reflect the tears of Apache squaws and others mourning the death of loved ones killed in an area battle.

Superior country, indeed, has novel attractions.

Picket Post House, built in 1923, at cost of $1,000,000 is open to visitors

KEARNY
the General's spirit lives on!

The spirit of Gen. Stephen Watts Kearny, U.S. Army General, who traveled through today's Pinal County more than 100 years ago, still pervades this community along State 177.

His picture enhances the lobby of the General Kearny Inn. His legendary life is heralded on a bronze plaque enshrined along Main Street and even on Inn menus.

How nice for a town to commemorate a patriot whose life was part and parcel of the early West!

The town is not a company town, per se, in that residents own their homes, business is privately owned and there is a mayor-council type government. But, the work force of the community is largely employed by Kennecott Copper Corp. In 1986, the open pit and mill were still in operation. The smelter was closed.

The town, founded in 1959, is relatively new. The company had the town constructed to house plant workers and their families, with many transplanted when the former town of Ray was abolished to expand the open pit Ray Mine.

The place is reached by veering on State 177 at Superior and heading south about 22 miles on a colorful desert-mountain swath.

Motorists know they are in Kennecott country when the recesses of the huge Ray Mine come in view. A billboard invites travelers to a viewpoint of the immense open pit operation. It is well worth the brief sashay off the highway.

At the Gen. Kearny Inn coffee shop, the menu with its Gen. Kearny story brings visitors into an historic mood.

At the outbreak of the Mexican War, it was President Polk who directed Kearny to organize the "Army of the West" to travel into Santa Fe in 1846, and to later secure California. Kearny claimed the area of Santa Fe for the U.S. and organized a civil government.

Kit Carson, frontiersman, served as his guide on the long march to California with 100 dragoons. An official log noted that on November 5 and 6, Kearny's group camped by the junction of the Gila and San Pedro rivers near today's Winkelman. On November 7, they journeyed down the Gila, camping near its junction with Mineral Creek, where the Ray Mine was located.

Gen. Kearny later became known as the "Father of the U.S. Cavalry." He died in 1848 at age 54 as result of a fever he contracted

Main street in mining-based town of Kearny

during his service in Mexico.

The town's real heritage, of course, is in mining. A Porter Air Locomotive enshrined along Main Street was used by Kennecott in the original underground Ray Copper Mine to transport men, ore and supplies underground. Operated on compressed air supplied from lines within the mine, it was retired in 1955, and later presented as a gift to the town.

Kearny, at elevation 2020 ft. boasts a residential area of nice homes, several churches, an elementary and high school. Some homes and at least one church were transplanted from Ray. The main business street was marked with concrete boxes of petunias in a bevy of colors, an attractive municipal touch.

If there is time, visitors may want to see the nearby Ray Memorial Cemetery, where graves were transplanted from old Ray.

Unusual tombstones mark the barren park dotted with many little metal disks that simply state: "UNK" for unknown.

Most markers are simple concrete cubicles, identical in size, bearing the name and dates of birth and death. A large white marble headstone is inscribed in big letters: "Tommy Hogay Left Us in November 1926." There must be no other cemetery exactly like this one.

For an outsider, the night here seemed quiet. The "in" thing was to head for dinner at the Kearny Inn.

Townspeople gathered for Saturday night dinner. The camaraderie was evident as friends "table hopped" in greetings. Knowing the populace is a bonus for small-town living.

Some chatted about the annual benefit tea by the Friends of the

Library to take place the next day at the home of the mine manager "at the top of the hill." It was to be a social event of the season.

Outside, the full moon had risen over Dripping Springs Hills, clothing the town and the Tortilla Mountains in a spectacular illumination.

It was pleasant, indeed, to spend a night in Kearny.

A viewpoint look at Kennecott Copper Corporation's Ray Mine

MAMMOTH
first gold—then copper!

Big plus for this mining-born town is its panoramic view of the Galiuro Mountains, brilliant in the afternoon sun, purple-hazy in the early morning.

Five years since observing its centennial founding date, 1876, Mammoth sprawled along Arizona 77, paralleling in part its main street in the old part of town. Population (in 1984) was estimated at 1,960 and mining is still a factor since some Mammoth people are employed by mines in neighboring San Manuel.

The place got its name, some say, from a mammoth gold discovery. *Arizona Republic* files depict a version of the town's history.

It was about the mid-1870s that gold was discovered in this San Pedro Valley community and in the surrounding territory, in a region then known as the Old Hat Mining District. There were old camps, now not even ghost-town status—such as Copper Creek Camp—in the area.

The early gold strike was on the eastern slope of the Catalina Mountains, about four miles up the hill from Mammoth, and some 800 feet above the town, according to *Arizona Republic* files.

Mammoth, the town, came into being when a stamp mill was built beside the river, as there was a shortage of water at the mine.

By 1890, there were several hundred people living in Mammoth. There were stores, several saloons and a school house.

Disaster struck in April 1901, when there was an extensive cave-in at the mine. There was no loss of life, however.

Fortunately, molybdenum was discovered in mining tailings, and then there was the year of the oil rush in 1904. About that time, it was said, there was not a strip of "unlocated" land within 20 miles of Mammoth.

The oil rush did not last long and even the Mammoth Mine shut down. And, still more, the San Pedro frequently flooded, cutting into farming as part of the economy.

"By 1930, only a few good farms remained," wrote Lowell Parker of the *Arizona Republic.* "It looked in the 1930s like Mammoth had had it."

"What really brought the town back to its present proportions was the opening of the San Manuel Mine by the Magma Copper

Town Hall in "downtown" Mammoth

Co. and the building of a completely new town a few miles to the southeast. Mammoth became the home for copper miners, not gold seekers," he said.

The town, incorporated in 1958, is small but a pleasant night can be spent in Mammoth at the small, austere rooms, including a small television, at the Sierra Vista Motel. At the Redwood Inn restuarant, a T-Bone steak dinner cost $6.75 (in 1981), and an array of Mexican food was drawing brisk business.

Mammoth was quiet on a Saturday night. As a cafe patron said, "If people here really want a night out-on-the-town, they go to Tucson."

Obtaining breakfast on a Sunday morning was a different story, but the answer was found at the Circle K Store—hot coffee, canned juice and doughnuts.

Map of Southeast Arizona

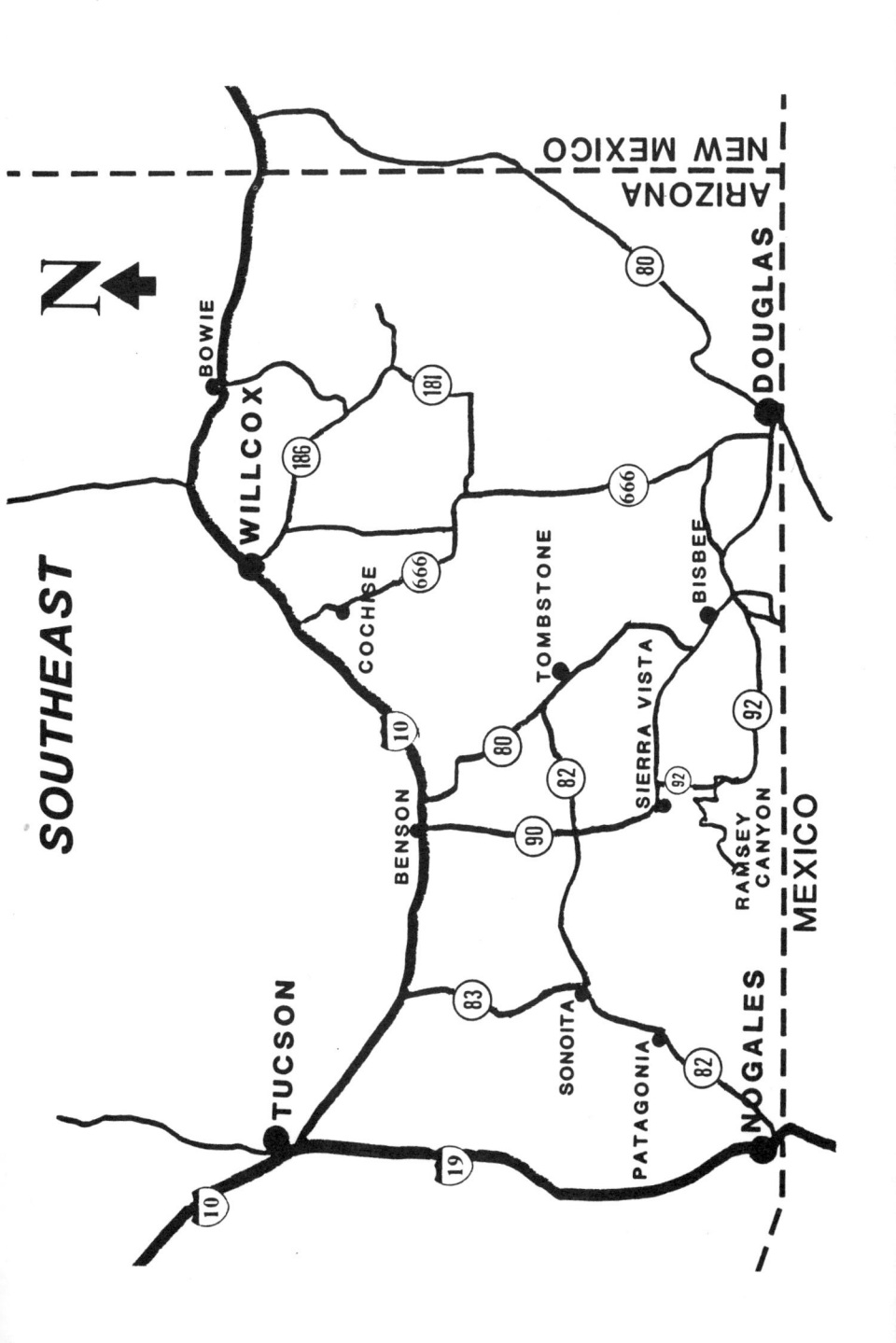

Centennial marker in Bowie near site of well dug in 1880 Bowie

BOWIE
friendly town, old fort!

It was 8 o'clock and the obviously popular restaurant was busy on an early September night.

A decorative sign on the wall said, "The nice part about a little town is that when I don't know what I'm doing, someone else does." A poster announced Diane's upcoming shower in the San Simon Fire Station.

The atmosphere manifestly was informal, friendly.

On a return visit, the restaurant name had changed to "Bill and Marie's Truck Stop," but the same spirit of camaraderie existed.

A counter sign urged "Support the Seniors" and listed upcoming events. Cookbooks, "Bowie's Favorite Recipes," were for sale for $5.

That's the charm of a little place. Strangers can immediately become interested.

Bowie, billed by the chamber of commerce as "in the Garden of the Sun," has a population hovering around 600, a citizen informed. It is along Interstate 10, in the southeast corner of Cochise County in the San Simon Valley, 28 miles from New Mexico.

The economy of the valley stems, the chamber notes, from the production of beef cattle, cotton, maize and fruit with irrigation water drawn from drilled wells.

In the Bowie area (altitude 3,765 ft.), effort is made to find a more lucrative product than cotton. Some 600 acres are already in pistachio trees with hope that the area can produce significant crops of the nut. Grapes, pecans, black-eyed peas are among other produce.

The town's major claim to tourist fame is old Fort Bowie some 13 miles south. The fort was established as an important military base in 1862 during the time when Indian wars were significant factors.

Pistachio trees growing in Bowie

On July 28, 1862, a 100-man detachment of the Fifth California Volunteer Infantry began construction of Fort Bowie. Two and a half weeks later, the rag-tag fort was completed. A 4-ft. wall, 412 ft. long, surrounded a collection of tents and a stone guard house.

Shortly after Geronimo's final surrender in 1886, Ft. Bowie's useful life as a military post ended. Fragments of the old buildings now constitute a National Historic Site administered by the National Parks Service.

The fort required a 1.5 mile walk, along a trail that boasts a post cemetery, remains of the Butterfield Stage Station and interesting flora.

The scenic Chiracahua National Monument with its famed Wonderland of Rocks is about 32 miles from Bowie.

Bowie, the town, came into being (according to *Arizona Place Names*) after Capt. James Tevis, who had served with Confederate forces in the 1860s with the Arizona Scouts, returned later to homestead in the area. A pen-and-ink picture of Tevis hung on the wall of the Bowie Justice of the Peace Court.

Tevis donated ground for the Cochise Milling Co. A post office was suggested so that mail would not have to be brought from Fort Bowie.

The Yucca Motel Lodge was selected from a phone directory for an overnight stop, largely because of its advertised "Let us make you at Home." The room was clean, comfy and at a conservative price. Not far away was another motel, "Home on the Range."

At Bill and Marie's, a roast pork dinner complete with salad bar and dessert was a mere $3.50—and tasty.

An unincorporated town, Bowie encompasses elementary and high schools, justice court, clinic, two motels, volunteer fire department and a 32-member chamber of commerce.

Bowie celebrated its centennial in 1980. A neat sign in a yard at Railroad and Eisenhower avenues told the story:

> Close to this site in July 1880, Capt. James H. Tevis, M. E. Kinchilla, A. Evans, J. Navaretta dug a well to 80 feet, finding water. The town was founded . . . Sign erected by citizens of Bowie, July 4, 1980.

Bowie residents consider Tevis the founder of the town. The Desert Rest Cemetery, marked by tall cypress and huge cedars, contains his tomb.

Leaving town, it seemed fitting to buy a bag of pistachio nuts from a nearby Stuckey's store. The pistachio flavor and memories of Bowie combined pleasantly.

Bowie historic old school building

COCHISE
family-style living!

Travelers daring to be different may want to experience a night in the Cochise Hotel, a hostelry steeped in Arizona's own brand of history.

Bedrooms boast high ceilings, marble-topped dressers, brass bedsteads and, for atmosphere, pitchers and bowls. No television.

Family-style dinners were served at a prescribed hour and afterwards, guests gathered around the upright piano and sang.

Who needs television in such a get-away place?

Some elect to sit on the beige plush sofa that reputedly belonged to Jenny Lind. There's a windup phonograph and a bookcase with such oldies as Elsie Dinsmore volumes and Owen Wister's *The Virginian*.

The hotel never advertises. Travelers learn by word of mouth or through stories about the place. You can't just walk in off the street and expect to spend the night or eat a meal. Both require advance reservations.

People who drive to the Southern Arizona place don't expect an ultra modern establishment. They anticipate an unusual night and is w from the minute the threshold is crossed they are in for a cozy experience.

Without television, most guests snuggle in bed early and let the quietness of the place sift about them. Never mind that the Southern Pacific freight trains do charge through Cochise. That, too, is part of the atmosphere.

And, by the way, the pitchers and bowls really are for decor. Each bedroom or suite has its own bath. The hotel has sleeping accommodations for 12.

Biggest ingredient is the hotel's age and history. Cochise, named for the famed Chiracahua Apache Indian Chief, is 85 miles east of Tucson and four miles south of Interstate 10 on Route 666, west of Willcox. It is in a quiet setting, not far from Cochise Stronghold.

The community's history wrapped around such milestones as the establishment of the railroad station here in 1887 (according to *Arizona Place Names*), the post office in 1886 and a Wells Fargo Station, 1903. A hotel was needed when train passengers stepped off the train for a night's rest. The hotel opened with beds and rooms, but the "new" addition—the kitchen and dining room—

came along in the 1890s.

The hotel was acquired in 1959 by Mrs. Thomas (Elizabeth) Husband, who launched a restoration program.

Research is underway to establish the exact date of the hotel's founding. Some contend it was established as early as 1881, some in the early 1890s. Mrs. Husband believes in the 1882 date.

People who come to the hotel do not care whether its vintage is 1882 or 1892. It is an historic place.

A plaque in the kitchen denotes the U.S. Department of Interior has placed the hotel on the National Register of Historic Places.

Guests enter via the back door with its welcoming sign, "Come In." The front door is locked.

During a 1982 visit, the oak dining table, stretched with seven leaves and lighted with chandelier, was an inviting setting for nine diners and their lively conversation.

The plain but delicious fare ($6.95) included a half chicken per serving, bowls of mashed potatoes and butter, peas, cornbread muffins, coffee and chocolate sundaes.

Lillie Harrington manages the hotel with precision. When she says dinner will be served at 6 p.m., she means it. That goes for her announcement, too, that bacon and eggs would be "laid on the table" at 7 a.m., for breakfast.

Cochise Hotel offers cozy experience

Country store across from Cochise Hotel

Mrs. Harrington and the old hotel go together famously. Both have colorful, engaging personalities. Long ago, Mrs. Harrington helped her husband drive a band of 38 untamed horses across a wide swath of Arizona.

The unincorporated community includes a Country Store, antique shop, the hotel gift shop and a school.

Reservations may be made by calling or writing to the Hotel, P.O. Box 27, Cochise, AZ 85606.

BENSON
loud echoes in passing rails!

A Southern Pacific freight train zoomed through town radiating vibrations, but diners at the Horseshoe Restaurant never lifted an eyebrow.

It's apropos that Fourth Street paralleling the railroad tracks here is the main drag. Benson and railroads grew up together. Historians note, in fact, that Benson stemmed from the advent of the SPRR in 1880.

The town, which already has celebrated its centennial, was named for Judge William Benson, who was involved many years in western mining regions and was a friend of the railroad president.

The town, incorporated in 1924, is often hailed as "The Gateway to Cochise County." Located 45 miles east of Tucson, off Interstate 10, Benson, according to its chamber of commerce, has gained favor as a retirement and bedroom community.

At the Horseshoe Restaurant, a patrolman—neat in crisp uniform—stopped in for an evening meal and relaxing respite. In a chat, he suggested Zearing's Mercantile Americana store as an interesting place for newcomers and strangers to learn about the town.

There are several motels and restaurants in Benson. And, for the stranger, window-gazing along Fourth Street reveals surprises.

Several buildings bore historical labels. The placard at The

Early commercial building in Benson

Sign marks historic event

Apparel Shop, said "Joseph Goldwater, great-uncle of Senator Goldwater, had a store here in 1887," and the sign at Hi Wo Co. Grocery, proclaimed "Hi Wo (Chinese) bought this building in 1896."

Most sensational was the placard notice in the H & R Block Building: "Site of the Wildcat Saloon. Jack the Ripper (Barkeep) shot to death here in 1906."

The Fashion Nook boasts a window marker, too: "Site of Zeke's Barbership in 1896 when floods washed away homes, drowning wife and two children."

Benson, obviously, loves its history.

Visitors should stop at the museum and gift shop operated by the San Pedro Arts and Historical Society, 142 S. San Pedro St.

The museum has exhibited both historical and artistic displays and produced historical calendars. The society museum is operated by volunteers. Boutique items are on consignment and a few antique items also are for sale.

The museum is housed in a building constructed in the 1920s as a grocery store. For many years, it was boarded up in disuse.

Museum hours are 10-4 Tuesday through Friday, 10-2 Saturdays and 2-4 Sundays.

Downtown Benson

The Amtrak "depot" in Benson

74 BENSON (Southeast Arizona)

San Pedro Valley Arts and Historical Society Museum in Benson welcomes visitors

Cars at The Sahara, a comfortable motel stop for the night, were from states ranging from Maryland to Montana.

A musical tape played "Red Wing" the next morning at Zearing's. Visitors who migrated into its Old Candy Store section were in for a sweet-tooth experience.

Wally Zearing handed out enticing sample chocolate balls with such delectable flavors as mandarin orange liqueur, cognac and rum. Even the jellybeans were not run-of-the-mill affairs. They came in 30 flavors. Whopper jawbreakers—made for licking—were also available.

There was much more than candy. The mercantile included such wares as jewelry, knives, guns, oil lamps, posters, iron spurs, bottles.

Things were appropriately quiet during a visit in the Benson Library, with a sign "Everyone's talking about our new books."

A prominent volume was titled "How to Recycle Old Clothes into New Fashions."

Everywhere, it seemed, Bensonites were friendly and cordial.

The historic depot is gone. Instead, passengers can wait at a little shed for the Amtrak that comes through town twice a day.

Several historic points within a not-too-far radius of Benson include Tombstone, some 26 miles away, Pearce and Gleeson.

BISBEE
a living history!

Bisbee is a showpiece in history, an exercise in nostalgia.

The aura begins the moment one tops a road in Mule Mountains and looks down on a panorama of yesteryear buildings, tiered on the hillside. They range from the draw of Tombstone Canyon to downtown old Bisbee and Brewery Gulch.

History is reflected from the old Phelps Dodge Mercantile building completed in 1895 and now the home of the Bisbee Mining and Historical Museum to the Pythian Lodge, circa 1904—its clock tower a prominent pinnacle.

The aura of the old is wrapped around the three-story post office building, with the city's Copper Queen Library on the third floor reached by 48 steps. The tall spire of the Covenant Presbyterian Church, beckoning at 19 Howell Ave., was dedicated in 1903 when a 579 pipe organ was installed.

Visitors can steep themselves in the old, the historic, by taking a 32-station self-guided walking tour on Main, Subway, Opera, Howell, Brewery, Naco and O.K. streets.

To further satisfy the appetite for the old, there is a tour of the old Copper Queen Mine, an underground adventure into one of the most historic mines in the Southwest. The tour, where turn-of-the-century mining methods can be seen, traverses one level of the old mine tunnel. Mine tour-takers should dress warmly, as the mine has a constant temperature of 47 degrees.

The Lavender Pit, its stripping operation for copper starting in 1951, lived until the mid 1970s. The pit encompassed 300 acres and was mined in 50 ft. benches. One statistic indicates that approximately 79 million tons of waste were mined for a total of 351 million tons of materials.

Bisbee is old.

It all began, historians note, after discovery of rich ore by three Army Scouts camped in Mule Pass in 1877. One later grubstaked the work of George Warren. Then Judge Dewitt Bisbee, a San Francisco investor, entered the mining picture in Mule Gulch. Phelps Dodge and Dr. James Douglas acquired mining property and in 1880 merged mining efforts to form the Copper Queen Consolidated Mining Co.

Downtown Bisbee street scene—complete with "B" on mountain

(Southeast Arizona) BISBEE 77

Interestingly enough, *Arizona Place Names,* which lists name origins, notes that Bisbee, a shareholder in Copper Queen Consolidated, never visited the town that bore his name.

Artists, jewelry-makers, potters and poets (there is an annual poetry festival in August billed as a "literary feast") call Bisbee home. The Bisbee area, including Warren, Lowell and San Jose communities, also attract retirees to the relative quiet of the near mile-high area.

One of the biggest adventures is spending the night in the Copper Queen Hotel. Built in 1902 by the Copper Queen Mining Co. (later Phelps Dodge Corp.), the four-story hotel—anchored firmly to a hillside—is said to have hosted Teddy Roosevelt, "Black Jack" Pershing, territorial governors, John Wayne and mining executives. The hotel was restored by private ownership.

The hotel dining room, with its evening-time white cloth-covered tables, features a good cuisine served with decorum. Chandeliers with teardrop crystal pendants and ornate wall pictures add to the charm.

Visitors can savor the charm of the quaint old elegance of the hotel with its high ceilings, red brocade-patterned papered hallways, and friendly staff. And, there is the startling head of a buffalo (killed in 1952 at the Ft. Huachuca Buffalo Range) hanging in the second story lobby.

Another historic structure is Anthony's Restaurant, now housed in the old Phelps Dodge Mercantile Building, constructed in 1938. The building has been remodeled and modernized as the Cleveland

Covenant Presbyterian Church dedicated in 1903

Historic Copper Queen Hotel in Bisbee

E. Dodge Center, through the Industrial Development Authority of the City of Bisbee.

Bisbee, the seat of Cochise County, is about 94 miles southeast of Tucson and ten miles from the Mexican border. There are several restaurants and bed-and-breakfast hostelries. The Bisbee Chamber of Commerce provides information.

Visitors browse around the winding streets, visiting old buildings. Bookstores with old books draw fans, while art galleries, the Mulheim House and museums attract others.

Brewery Gulch is a part of "Old Bisbee." A remnant of Bisbee's rowdy days, the gulch was the scene of freespending miners, saloons galore and "friendly" ladies.

Near the courthouse, built in 1931, a statue of a man in gleaming copper is dedicated to the "Virile men, the copper miners whose contributions to the wealth and lore of the state have been magnificent."

History is the big drawing card. Even business places capitalize on the past.

At "The Flapper," a modern dress shop at 18 Main St., for instance, tile flooring outside the door has a unique sign that says, "On this site in 1897, nothing happened."

RAMSEY CANYON
—where you are Nature's guest!

"Please help our birds and other wildlife by whispering, staying on the trail and being polite. You are a guest of nature."

The sign sets the tone for The Nature Trail that criss-crosses Ramsey Creek, high in the Huachuca Mountains.

The creek babbles unceasingly. There were shoulder-high yellow

Creek babbles through Mile Hi area

daisies and an assortment of white, blue and lavender flowers plus butterflies galore. And, in mid-September, old apple trees were laden with pink-red fruit.

Benches at observation points along the three-quarter mile round-trip offered a chance to "sit a spell" and absorb the beauty. Along the path, forest, desert and riparian vegetation mingle. There are a medley of forest trees and wild grapevines, and, in a delicate moment, a deer watched from a distance.

"The trail you are on will take you through some very fragile wildlife areas," the sign continues. "Birds are nesting near the trail everywhere. They need their home quiet and undisturbed."

The idea sinks in. Birds and nature get high priority in the Mile Hi/Ramsey Canyon Preserve. A trail guide brochure, which may be purchased at the bookstore, cites the emory oaks, the spiny evergreen buckbrush and cautions about rattlesnakes.

Fifteen species of hummingbirds have been noted here, but there is ke to browse, even poison ivy, also a variety of other birds—flycatchers, warblers, wrens and woodpeckers, to name a few.

Ramsey Canyon contains notably diverse flora and fauna, much of which is more characteristic of the Sierra Madre Mountains of Mexico than of the U.S., a bulletin board notes. In the canyon area, there is a tremendous variety of birds, mammals, amphibians, reptiles and butterflies. Ramsey Canyon preserve is managed so that the community of plants and animals, in which each plays a part, shall remain undisturbed.

In an effort to conserve a portion of this unique area, The Nature Conservancy, a national conservation organization, established a 300-acre preserve along Ramsey Canyon in 1975. The Nature Conservancy was incorporated in 1951 for scientific and educational

Along the nature trail in Ramsey Canyon

purposes. The Conservancy has been responsible for preservation of more than two million acres in forests, marshes, prairies, mountains and islands in the U.S.

Ramsey Canyon in southern Arizona is reached by traveling six miles south of Sierra Vista on State 92 to the well-marked Ramsey Canyon Road. Mile Hi, locale of the cabins and hummingbird feeders, is gained after four miles on the canyon road (the last 200 yards is dirt).

April through September are the best birding months at Mile Hi, but amateur naturalists can find much of interest in the canyon and vicinity the year around. People come here, some 15,000 a year, to spend a night in a cabin or sit beneath a tree-shade canopy to observe and photograph the hummers as they zoom to dangling feeders.

The six furnished cabins are nestled among the giant sycamores and gamboling squirrels. Overnight guests need only bring food for the stay. The "Creek Cabin," for instance, offered a bedroom combination living, dining and kitchen area plus bath. There is no television, but a steak barbecue in the privacy of the front yard is a treat. And, the chattering creek can lull you to sleep at night.

In 1983, the Mile Hi area experienced flash flood problems due to an earlier fire in the Upper Ramsey Canyon that destroyed ground cover growth. The burned area is now recovering.

Day visitors may obtain passes for the trail hike at no cost from the office, 8 a.m. to 5 p.m. No picnicking facilities are offered day visitors. The small parking area cannot accommodate RVs over 20 feet. There are only eight parking spots.

On up the canyon, some 2½ miles from Mile Hi, are remains of the old Hamburg Mine.

Mile Hi, at 5525 feet altitude, is open the year around. Most of the hummingbird population, depending on the weather, leave sometime in September and return late in March.

The Mile Hi Bookstore contains an extensive collection of bird books, nature books, bird slides, postcards and note paper, and helps support the work of The Nature Conservancy.

Because of very limited parking, weekday visits are recommended. Advance phone reservations are required for all visits on Saturdays, Sundays and federal holidays. Organized groups should contact the preserve in advance to schedule visits. Hours are 8 a.m. to 5 p.m. daily. Phone (602) 378-2785. Reservations for cabins, necessary to avoid disappointment, can be made by calling the same number.

For further information about the Conservancy, write the Arizona Nature Conservancy, P.O. Box 40236, Tucson, AZ 85717.

PATAGONIA
quiet attractions and horse museum

In the midst of verdant ranch country, the town of Patagonia stands as a focal point for excursions in southern Arizona.

Its position on State Route 82 leads into rolling hills and grasslands, and to Patagonia Lake and the Patagonia-Sonoita Creek Bird Sanctuary.

Tucson, Nogales, Tubac, an area ghost town circuit, and Tombstone lie within a scenic and enjoyable two-day motoring swing that offers pleasant overnight accommodations in Patagonia and even a hearty steak dinner at nearby Sonoita.

The area abounds in quiet attractions. On Route 82, the Nogales road, there is an unmarked shrine from World War II that is still maintained. About five miles out of town, the shrine is approached by a quaint stairway up a steep incline. Little religious statues and flickering candles in glass bases bear testimony to the shrine's patronage. A gate is intended to discourage vandalism.

A Patagonian explained the shrine. During World War II a mother vowed that if her four sons returned from battle "alive and well" she would build the roadside shrine. They returned safely, and in 1945 the mother dedicated the small shrine.

Patagonia, incorporated in 1948, and with a population in 1986

Old railroad station serves as Patagonia's municipal building

84 PATAGONIA (Southeast Arizona)

of about 1045, has its corner on nostalgia. The Cady Hall Patagonia Hotel, built in 1900, no longer takes boarders, but has been converted into the town library and Patagonia Women's Club home. Today the traveler may stay at the Stage Stop Inn and dine at the Feed Lot Restaurant, quenching his thirst at the Last Gap Saloon.

The town's big attraction, too, is the Stradling Museum of the Horse, Inc., established in 1960, housing a collection of life-size horse statuary, saddles, art work and an array of carriages, buggies, surreys and even a Conestoga Wagon.

The nearby bird sanctuary boasts cottonwood trees 100 feet tall. More than 200 species of birds dart over Sonoita Creek, home of aquatic animals as well as deer and bobcat. It is a place to visit silently. As of 1980, no camping or picnicking was permitted.

Route 82 offers peace and tranquility through historical terrain where U.S. troops and Indians once battled. Motorists can see old Fort Crittendon remains from the highway.

Sonoita's Steak Out restaurant is that town's most visible attraction. Here, again in 1980, you could dine on a two-pound porterhouse steak, beef filet or jumbo sirloin broiled over a mesquite fire in an inside fireplace.

There is hardly a better way to sample the springtime exhilaration of the wide-open western roads than down Patagonia way.

Birdwatching in Patagonia-Sonoita Creek Sanctuary

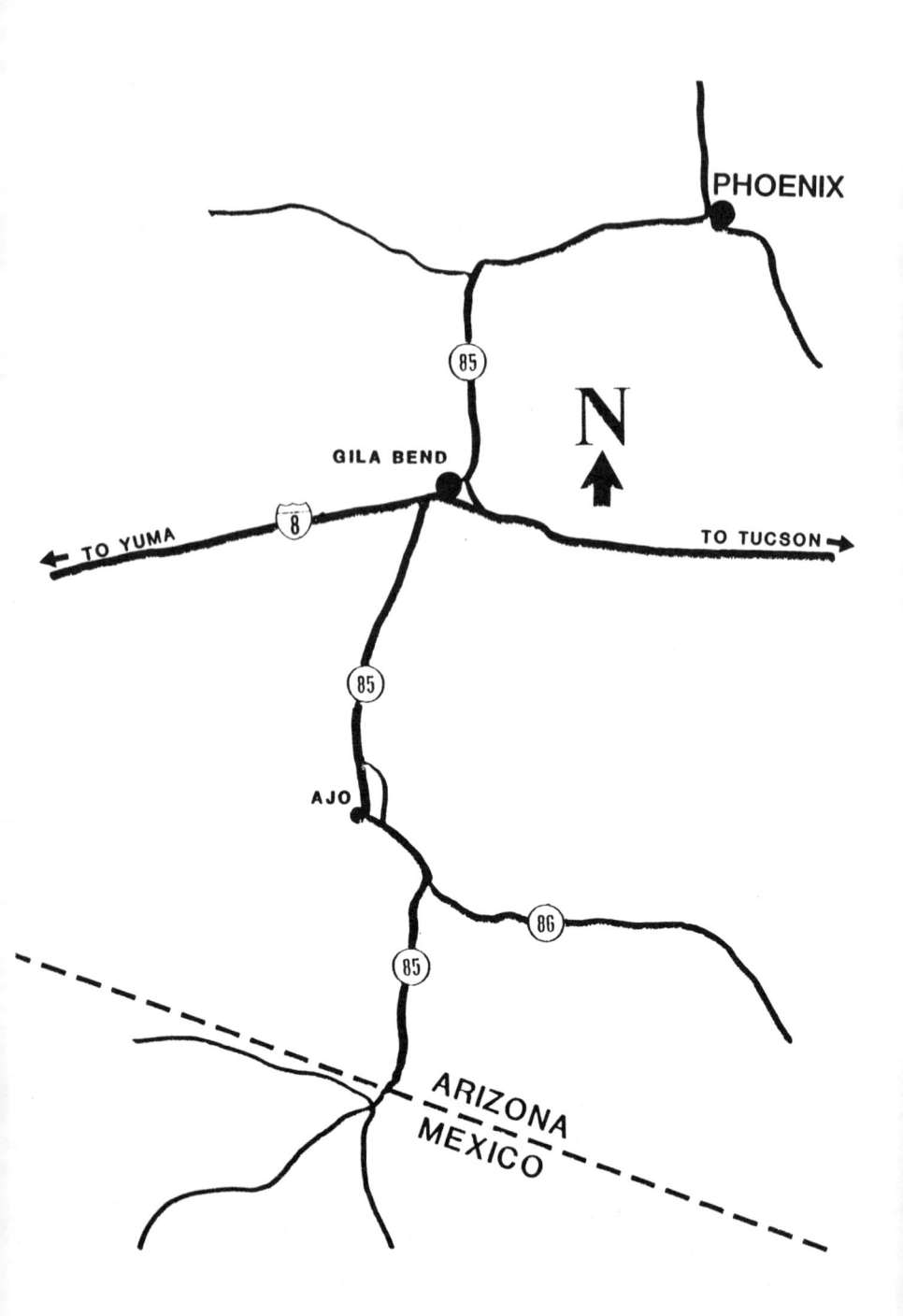

SOUTHWEST

Quaint sign greets visitors entering Gila Bend

GILA BEND
where the sun spends the winter!

    Never mind that this town sizzles in the summertime or that it is sometimes the hot spot in the nation.
    Citizens here are well aware that El Sol generates torrid temps. In fact, in the wintertime, it capitalizes on the sun.
    Witness a town motto adopted by the Gila Bend Chamber of Commerce: "Where the sun spends the winter."
    Nobody can say exactly when travelers first came into Gila Bend, surrounded by desert, saguaro cacti and mountains. But, it was eons ago.
    Gila Bend fans can point with pride to the town's rich historic past.
    Archaeologists say Indians came up from the peninsula of Baja, California, along the Colorado until it joined the Gila River, then journeyed up the river to the northern mountains.
    Later, historians note, Father Eusebio Kino, great Spanish missionary, named an Indian settlement on the big bend of the Gila Uparsoytas, in about 1700. Then there were the French traders around 1827 and the Mormon Battalion that passed through in 1847, opening the way to the coast.
    Historians cite the Butterfield Stage that brought the first scheduled mail here in October 1858. The town, in fact, celebrates

the event annually in the Butterfield Stage Fiesta Days in October.

There is much more to the town's history. The Gila Bend Chamber of Commerce likes to tell the story about the time a cyclone struck the town.

According to chamber information, a cyclone struck the town in 1898. The world thought the settlement was wiped out. A week later, the story goes, word reached the outside world and people knew Gila Bend was still itself.

The first words—an order for eight barrels of beer!

A sign on the outskirts of the town, off Interstate 8: "Gila Bend Welcomes You. Home of 1700 friendly people and five old crabs." Gila Bend residents encountered were friendly. The five cranky persons may have left town.

Gila Bend's low building profile basked brightly on an October 1985 day. The temperature crept to 84 degrees.

At the Gila Bend Community Center, noon lunch was in preparation for a food program there. The Gila Bend Public Library was open in another area of the complex built in 1982.

In a reconverted building, the town hall on Pima, the main drag through town, opened in modern quarters a few months ago. In the council chambers, red and blue lights signal the yes and no votes of councilmen. The Gila Bend town flag (how many towns have a town flag?) reflects the town's history and was designed by John Laird, a former councilman.

Other buildings mark headquarters for the Gila Bend Volunteer Fire Department and elsewhere were offices of the Maricopa County Sheriff's office deputies, who provide police protection for the town.

Gila Bend's modern community center and library complex

Petroglyphs invite inspection at Painted Rocks State Historic Park

Motels, restaurants, service stations and grocery marts line along the Pima thoroughfare. At Andy's V & S Variety Store, shoppers browsed among the myriad of merchandise.

Expanding agriculture and a growing military base, the Gila Bend Auxiliary Air Field and gunnery range are factors in the local economy. Since Gila Bend is located on major routes connecting Phoenix and Tucson with Yuma and the Pacific Coast, the place is a popular overnight stop for travelers.

Gila Bend is also the gateway to Ajo and Organ Pipe Cactus National Monument. Some 15 miles away, Painted Rock Historic Park boasts an outstanding collection of petroglyphs.

State park information notes that the "meaning of the petroglyphs is known only to those who made them. Some may be 1000 years old. Landforms like these basalt boulders were often held in respect by early people."

A self-service pay station at the park indicated the nominal daily fee required per vhicle. There are ramadas and picnic facilities but no water at the site. Painted Rock Dam Lakes are about four miles away.

Near Gila Bend are the Gatlin Ruins of the Ho-Ho-Kam Indians. The Gatlin Ruins, named for a local rancher, is a site leased by the State of Arizona to the town. The National Register of Historic Places has listed the Gatlin site as highly significant.

The town with its historic past was named long ago for its location at a bend in the Gila River.

Memorabilia down AJO way!

The downtown plaza park, heart of this remote mining town, basked in patterns of sunshine and shade.

On a warm February morning, visitors and townspeople roamed the park, rested on park benches or traipsed beneath the Spanish arches facade of plaza stores.

The Ajo Federated and Immaculate Conception Churches, in snow white exteriors, loomed like twin bastions of faith in this town born of mining.

The post office, zip 85321, was busy and the Phelps Dodge Mercantile was drawing a share of shoppers. Cars were banked in most parking slots around the park.

A giant "A" on the mountain that presides over the area bespoke of community identity and pride, and towering far above on the mountain's peak, a white cross was profiled against the azure sky.

At one time, eighth grade graduating students scaled the mountain to whitewash and restore the "A."

Ajo is located along State Highway 85, just 42 miles south of Gila Bend and some 34 miles north of the Mexico border.

Newcomers need not seek out old history books to learn about the town's early history. Exterior plaques in front of the Pima County Building capsule the story.

> The City of Ajo, one says, was located first on ground that later became the open pit mine. The modern city was founded in its present location in 1917 coincident with the beginning of large scale mining of copper deposits.
>
> Ajo is the home of the Phelps Dodge New Cornelia Mine, which is one of the great copper mines in the world. The open pit mine is located one mile south of the city and the concentrator, smelter and shops are adjacent to the town site on the east.

The information helps visitors absorb the tone of the community.

The open pit mine lookout, wreathed in colors of beige, pinks and purple, is worth a visit. Benches are arranged where spectators can leisurely observe the fascinating pit.

Leaving the plaza on La Mina Road and veering on to Indian Village Road, it is not too far to the former St. Catherine's Mission, which now houses the Ajo Historical Society Museum.

An old ore cart, metates, a hose cart, old bells and olive trees, reportedly brought in from the Holy Land by priests, entice visitors.

Former Indian mission, now home of Ajo Historical Society Museum

Inside, two large rooms contain a maze of memorabilia—a 45-star flag, a typewriter "made between 1874 and 1900," period clothing, old tools, a rock collection, pictures galore and even an August 15, 1945, ***Arizona Republic,*** headlining the Japanese surrender ending World War II.

Commemorative plates, backed with significant dates in Ajo history and produced by the historical society, cost $6.25.

"The church building had been abandoned," the curator said. "The historical society needed a home. They got the church."

Back at the Pima County Building, another historical plaque sets forth information about the Ajo mining district:

> Americans first worked copper deposits at Ajo in 1854. One year after the Gadsden Purchase, these early Americans found abandoned workings and crude mining tools as mute evidence of early mining in the district.
>
> During the next half century, mining was confined to veins and other small deposits of high grade copper ore. Some ore was transported by mule train across the desert to Yuma for shipment (around Cape Horn) to Swansea Wales . . .

The New Cornelia Copper Co. plant went into operation in May 1917, initiating large-scale exploration of the Ajo copper deposits, the plaque notes.

The Greenway mansion, atop a hill towering above Indian Village Road, is a showplace and now the home of the Knights of Columbus. Newcomers may wonder about the significance of the Greenway name.

Again, an historical plaque, this time in the downtown plaza park, tells part of the story:

> John C. Greenway—the modern town of Ajo was laid out by this accomplished mining engineer who came to Arizona in 1910 to manage the Calumet and Arizona mines. Recognizing the potential value of low grade copper ore, he developed this pit mine. Later, as general manager of the New Cornelia Mining Co., he constructed the Tucson, Cornelia and Gila Bend railroad . . . Greenway died in 1926 and is buried in Ajo.

The town of Ajo, which in 1980 had a population of 5,189, stretches over a long area. During a 1983 visit, tables at the high-ceiling Copper Coffee Shop were festooned in the evening with candles flickering in blue glass vases. The menu indicated steaks, chicken, pork chops and a selection of Mexican food featuring tasty shredded beef.

Accommodations for two at La Siesta Motel were $24.72.

Downtown plaza in Ajo

Greenway hilltop mansion in Ajo

Tahono Arts, a neat shop along Highway 85, contained handcrafted items.

>(The Phelps Dodge Co. has since closed its mining operation here. Preliminary steps have been taken so that the company can sell some 600 company homes. The PD Mercantile store, motels, restaurants and other stores were open in early 1986.)

As a scenic bonus down Ajo way, there is the Organ Pipe Cactus National Monument. The magnificent reserve of virgin desert growth, crossed by Fernando Diaz in 1541, is 34 miles south of Ajo on Highway 85 that winds through beautiful Sonora Desert country.

In February, the desert beauty is heightened. Hillsides are riotously splashed with Mexican gold poppies.

Immaculate Conception Church in Ajo viewed from plaza arch

AJO (Southwest Arizona)

Map of Western Arizona

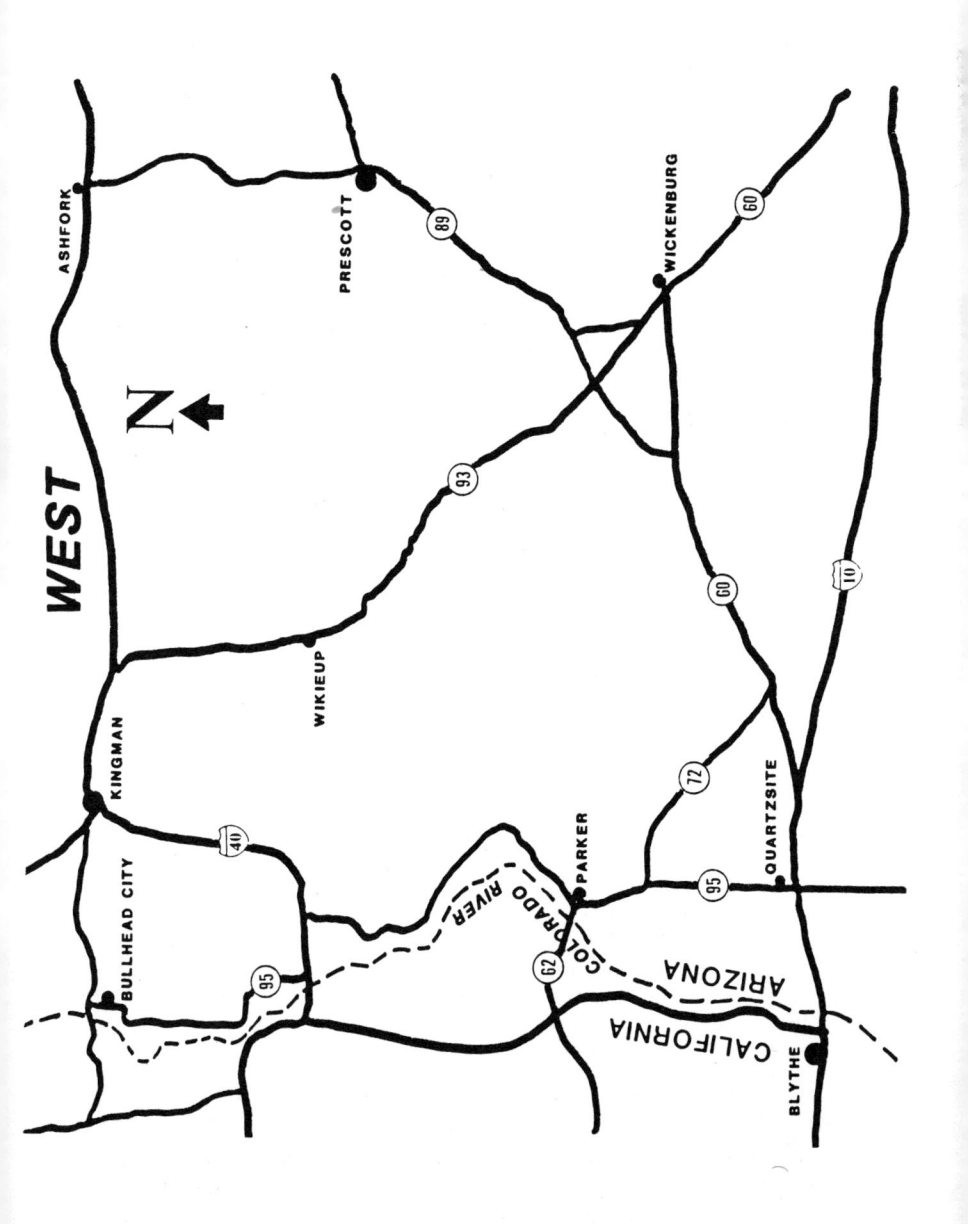

Out WICKENBURG way!
America's dude ranch capital!

Anchored in rolling foothills and wrapped in an aura of the Old West, this small city provides a one-of-a-kind visit among Arizona cities.

From one end of the town of about 5000 population to the other are reminders of its souvenir past.

The evidence speaks for itself.

Right off the bat and marking the bridge spanning the Hassayampa River, there is the sign, "No fishing from the bridge." Never mind that below the bridge the riverbed often is mostly dry.

Then, soon after crossing the river, there is the Wishing Well historical marker including the legendary reminder that those who drink the river's water will never tell the truth.

Consider the next, the ancient "Jail Tree," perhaps a token of early-day justice, in the center of the town. Apparently, before the town could afford a jail, the mesquite tree was an anchor where the non law-abiding could be chained. The sign: "From 1863 to 1890 outlaws were chained to this tree for lack of a hoosegow. Escapees were unknown."

Beyond Wickenburg on Highway 60, there's a Massacre Monument where ill-fated passengers on November 5, 1871, aboard a Wickenburg-Ehrenberg stage were ambushed. Marker date—1937.

Elsewhere, visitors may gain capsule information about the town via a plaque-bearing rocky monument to Henry Wickenburg. The weatherbeaten memorial, dedicated November 26, 1941, tells the story:

> The discoverer of the fabulously rich Vulture Mine and the man for whom the town of Wickenburg was named came to Arizona as a prospector in 1862.
>
> Legend tells us that this intrepid frontiersman, native of Prussia, found the Vulture gold in chunks of rocks he was throwing at a recalcitrant burro. Development of the mine led to milling activities along the Hassayampa River and subsequent growth of Wickenburg...

(According to information from the Wickenburg Chamber of Commerce, the Vulture Mine is now closed to the public.)

Much more can be learned about Wickenburg and vicinity through a visit to the showpiece Desert Caballeros Western Museum, that is billed as 14,000 sq. ft. of history. The museum is

"No Fishing" from Wickenburg's Hassayampa River Bridge

closed on Mondays and there is an admission fee.

Museum information relates that as the Vulture Mine grew, tradesmen came to service the workers. At first, there were itinerant merchants selling from the backs of their wagons, later from tents and buildings. Then came cattlemen, gardens, orchards and farms along the Hassayampa.

Later, and for decades, Wickenburg wore the hat "Dude Ranch Capital of the World," attracting people from throughout the country. Currently, there are five guest ranches in the area.

The Wickenburg Chamber capitalizes on the slogan "Out Wickenburg Way." Even car bumpers carry bright stickers themed, "Out Wickenburg Way."

The chamber is now housed in a new-old home, the restored Santa Fe Depot, vintage 1895, along Frontier Street. In January 1986, C of C coffee mugs, themed "Out Wickenburg Way," sold for $4.

Wickenburg was incorporated in 1909. Motorists, who merely drive through the town enroute to other destinations, are unaware of the neat, attractive city hall, and the nearby library and impressive-looking community center building. The library has information about early Wickenburg including a copy of "Out Wickenburg Way" and other cartoons that are the work of Cowboy Artist J. R. Williams.

Homey touches abound throughout the town.

In a residential area, a roadrunner may bound across the street at the approach of a car. And, at the Wickenburg Volunteer Fire Department, an overhead air siren sounds at the noon hour. Christmas carols pealed from the chimes at the St. Anthony Catholic Church during a cold December afternoon.

A variety of Wickenburg stores, some facades bespeaking a frontier atmosphere, attract shoppers. The variety ranges from a women's dress shop, "The Bustle"—labeled facetiously as "a deceitful seatful"—to antique stores. New construction has brought in the downtown Frontier Center and a Safeway-anchored shopping center on the highway.

At The Chaparral on Tegner Street, homemade breads, pastries and ice cream enticed shoppers. There are numerous motels and restaurants besides schools, churches and a hospital.

Tourism is obviously the most important business activity in Wickenburg economy. Reportedly there were 117 firms providing services to tourists.

The Gold Nugget Restaurant along Center, a main street, boasts a slogan in keeping with the town's ambience: "If you like Arizona, you'll love Wickenburg."

City Hall, Wickenburg, adorned with desert shrubbery

Old Santa Fe depot—new home of Wickenburg Chamber of Commerce

WICKENBURG (Western Arizona)

WIKIEUP
—for a change of pace!

Probably most people whiz through here bound to and from Kingman and Las Vegas, giving little thought to the fleeting village scene.

Some jaded motorists stop for coffee and a brief respite from the tiring mile after mile on U.S. Highway 93. Others are grateful for the chance to fill up gas tanks on the long haul.

But Wikieup's history fits a niche in Arizona lore, and travelers can tarry a while here over a steak dinner.

There is also a motel (we noticed only four rooms) and with advance reservations we did spend the night here. Tab for room for two at the Wikieup Motel was $20 (1981), with no radio or television facilities. However, the absence of news communications offered a change of pace and chance to see more of this remote place nestled near the Big Sandy River.

Of course, it doesn't take long to cruise up and down Wikieup's main strip, but at dinnertime we opted for Ola's Country Kitchen. We were not disappointed.

A small T-Bone steak dinner was a surprisingly low price and good. So were the coffee and service by Fern Meek, the waitress, who kept on the run as patrons gathered in for Sunday night dinner.

Remote Wikieup has its own post office

Wikieup, we were told, offers five cafes, a drive-in eatery, several garages—gasoline sales are a big item here—a bar, post office, two churches, a grocery store, variety store and small laundromat.

Antiques, including an interesting china closet, and lively conversation, claimed attention of patrons lingering over coffee cups at Ola's.

But, afterwards there was little to do except get a longer night's rest.

The next morning at breakfast, Mrs. Meek, who lived on a ranch near here in her childhood, talked about those days.

"We used to think it was drab here," she said. "But after work was done we would gather around and sing, play the guitar or a game of horseshoes."

Her father homesteaded near here and for a while she went to school at Signal, now a ghost town.

"It's still beautiful country," she said. "The atmosphere is clean and clear. The weather is not too hot in the summer, not real cold in the winter. Mining and cattle are our main resources. Many retired people have moved into the area."

Wikieup probably drew its name from reference to Indian built brush shelters. Life began to concentrate in this particular area of the Big Sandy Country around the turn of the century, but it wasn't until 1922 that Wikieup was chosen the name for the post office here.

There may be 400 people in the Wikieup area, but hundreds more pass daily through its portals, bent on other destinations.

BULLHEAD CITY
a dam—and casinos in view!

The Black Mountains, profiled in the early morning sun, background this remote river community in Arizona's far west.

In the valley below, the Colorado River rushes in a broad path between Bullhead City, Az., and Laughlin, Nev., and its gambling-casino shoreline.

Ferryboats, scurrying between the states, ply the river, providing fast conveyance for fun-bent gamblers. In a way, the free rides add adventure to casino visits.

Fishing, boating at Mohave Lake, the sparkling jewel of the desert that backs up Davis Dam about three miles upstream from here, and rock hunting in the nearby hills provide other diversions.

Visitors can either cross over Davis Dam by car and drive into Laughlin or ride ferryboats from Bullhead City docks to visit the casinos.

The Bullhead City area boasts several motels, and Laughlin also has casino hotel rooms.

The town came into being because of Davis Dam, and the earth-and-rock filled structure gave the area a big boost. Although construction started in August 1942, work was discontinued because of World War II. The dam was completed in 1953. Lake Mohave, behind the dam, is well-known to sportsmen.

Today, a visit to the dam (watch carefully at the State 68 'Y') can be an interesting side junket. A self-guided tour at the dam is worthwhile.

Hardyville, on the southern outskirts of Bullhead City and no longer even a ghost town, was a thriving steamboat landing more than 100 years ago. A rock memorial in front of The Sizzler Restaurant tells the story:

> William H. Hardy founded Hardyville in 1864. Hardyville remained an important mining, shipping and river crossing center to the turn of the 20th century. Many adobe buildings erected by Hardy stood here when the settlement started its existence as Hardy's Landing.

A remnant of Hardyville today is a forlorn patch of graves minus tombstones in the cemetery on a windswept bluff overlooking the Colorado River and busy State 95 highway.

Bullhead City is reached by State 68 out of Kingman or, for variety, a route along the Colorado River, State 95, from Parker

Ferryboat links Bullhead City, Arizona to Laughlin, Nevada, across Colorado River

and through Lake Havasu City.

A memorial at Bullhead City Community Park notes that commercial steamships on the Colorado were of great importance from 1852-1877.

Bullhead Rock, from which the town derived its name, was located upstream. The rock, known as a navigation mark along the Colorado, has been covered by waters of the dam since 1953.

The community, its population including many retirees, has gained national recognition as a summertime weather hot spot. The town has a newspaper, the "Mohave Valley News," and a 126-acre airport used basically by small airplanes and helicopters. (Residents voted to incorporate in 1984.)

On a Sunday morning at Holiday Plaza, a big tailgate sale was underway with wares ranging from homemade knit goods and jewelry to old coins, books and belt buckles.

Neon tubes brilliantly witness the casinos at night across the Colorado. During a January visit, a buffet supper in the glass-fronted dining room at Laughlin's Riverside Resort Hotel and Casino was enhanced by a novel night scene. A full moon cast a shimmering path on the Colorado.

PARKER
mile-square town on the Colorado

The little town of Parker, nestled in a far west recess near the Colorado River, is singular among Arizona municipalities.

Number one, it is a square mile in size, and secondly, it is surrounded on three sides by the Colorado River Indian Reservation. Furthermore, in January 1983, it became the seat of government for La Paz, Arizona's newest county.

And, although Parker's beginnings are dated much earlier (a post office established in 1871), its founding date is recorded as 1908. Incorporation came 40 years later.

The close-by, onrushing Colorado River, with the enticements of fishing, skiing, boating and tubing, is centerpiece of attraction to the Parker and reservation areas.

The Colorado River Indian Reservation lands are located in both La Paz County and California. Indian reservation administrative offices are located near Parker.

Encompassed in the Indian administration complex area is the Colorado River Indian Tribes Museum and Library, completed in 1966. Arts and crafts of the Mohave, Chemehuevi, Navajo and Hopi tribes are so museum. The interesting museum is dedicated to the culture and history of the Indian people.

The Colorado River Indian Reservation was established by an Act of Congress in 1865, at a time when it was the homeland of Mohave and Chemehuevi Indians. About 80 years later, Navajo and Hopi tribe members began living there. The reservation is considered unique because it is occupied by four tribes, each with its own culture and traditions.

Parker, at an elevation of 420 feet above sea level, is on the east bank of the Colorado River, some 162 miles northwest of Phoenix. Topping a mountain rise enroute on State 95, motorists find Parker lies beyond an expanse of lush green fields irrigated by mechanized water sprayers.

Agriculture is big in area economy, as well as tourism, the latter because of the Colorado River's sporting activity.

Parker Dam, about 15 miles northwest of the town along State Highway 95, spans the Colorado River between Arizona and California. Built between 1934 and 1938 by the Bureau of Reclamation, Parker Dam is said to be the "deepest" dam in the world. Seventy-three percent of its structural height is below the

Northern Yuma County Jail, built in 1914, is listed in National Register of Historic Places

original riverbed. Parker Dam is a part of a system of storage and diversion structures built by the bureau to control and regulate the once unruly Colorado River.

The power plant at Parker Dam is open to the public for self-guided tours at no charge seven days a week.

Short recorded lectures and other features make the tour educational and entertaining.

A drive a few miles north on State 95 from Parker offers glimpses of Colorado River beaches and waterside homes, both in Arizona and California.

The Parker area offers several motels, mobile and RV parks, two state parks and one county park. The Parker Area Chamber of Commerce is a source of information.

A new shopping mall, the Moovalya Plaza on Riverside is on the reservation, just outside the town limits. And, located in the town's Pop Harvey Park near the Parker Library is the old Northern Yuma County Jail built in 1914. The jail is listed on the National Register of Historic Places.

The Mohave Presbyterian Church, started in 1914 and finished in 1917, is an appealing sight on the reservation. It is also listed in the National Register.

The reservation museum notes that "the church not only was an instrument of Christianity but was a community center, which was the heart of tribal activities before the formation of the Colorado

River Indian Tribal Council."

Visitors found homey touches during a stay in Parker in a cool November sojourn.

And, in a thoughtful touch at the Kofa Inn Motel, a tiny card left by the bedside lamp along with two peppermints, said, "Thanks. You're worth a mint to us."

Parker's attractive public library

Church, on reservation, completed in 1917

QUARTZSITE
camaraderie among trailerites, rockhounds

Discovering Arizona happily can include a grassroots look at the little towns in remote places with Quartzsite an interesting case in point.

Quartzsite is off Interstate 10, about 19 miles from the California line. It's a haven in cooler months for trailer residents and rockhounds hailing from across the United States and Canada.

In the past, its most famous resident was Hadji Ali, more commonly known as "Hi Jolly," the famous camel driver, scout and packer. He served more than 30 years with the government and died in Quartzsite in 1902.

Visitors can see Ali's memorial, a pyramid shaped of stone, which was erected in 1935 by the Arizona Highway Department, on a rise west of town.

Once a year, thousands come to Quartzsite for the town's annual rock and gem powwow, usually in February. Then, the town and surrounding desert blooms with trailers and people.

The town's usual population—some residents in 1980 estimated about 300—bulges from October through March when retirees migrate here to bask and browse in the winter sun.

Swap meets and flea markets are the vogue, especially on Saturdays and Sundays. Sales reflect the ingenuity of an older segment of society trying to make a bit of money while enjoying life and independence.

Attractions include jewelry with turquoise and peridot, belt buckles and bola ties, Austrian crystal pendants, mobiles that catch the sun, hand-crocheted items, books, ironwood canes, clocks, lamps, rocks galore and sun hats.

After a morning browsing, a visiting foursome took stock of their purchases. There were a bag of agate rocks to tumble, $1.50 a pound; a Barry Goldwater for President political pin—vintage 1964, $1; a woman's plastic shade hat made in Taiwan, $3.50; a set of turquoise earrings for pierced ears, $5; two kewpie dolls (remember those days?) with crochet clothes, $3.75 each; and a polished geode, $2.

The purchases were not great treasures, but that's beside the point. It was fun acquiring them and talking to the friendly sellers.

Memorial to Hadji Ali (Hi Jolly) honors Arizona's famous camel driver

Most trailer residents are attracted here by the warm winter weather. The camaraderie among trailerites is another plus, a fan said. They pack up and move to cooler climates by April 1, but come next October or November, and most will be back again.

"It's like coming home," a trailerite confessed.

November is a month of big resurgence. After Christmas, more congregate. The rock show finds trailerites and visitors at the zenith season.

Quartzsite is located not far from the site of old Fort Tyson. *Arizona Place Names* says the fort was privately built and owned by Charles Tyson for protection against the Indians. Because of the availability of water, Tyson's Wells became a stage station on the road from Ehrenberg to Prescott.

For a time there was mining activity in the area, even a short-lived post office. Later when a new post office was opened, Quartzsite was suggested because of its availability in the area. It seemes that the post office made the mistake of adding the "s" to the name.

Hi Jolly was a camel driver for Lt. E. F. Beale on a trip across Arizona in 1857, according to an informative marker at the site.

Jefferson Davis, as secretary of war before he became president of the Southern Confederacy, approved a plan to experiment with camels for freighting and communications in the arid southwest.

The war department abandoned the experiment and the camels were left in the desert to shift for themselves, chiefly roaming a section including Quartzsite. They survived many years, creating interest and excitement.

In Quartzsite, there are two motels—the High Ali Hotel and the Stage Coach Inn. Clean and comfortable accommodations for two at the Stage Coach were $18.72 a night (1980). A top sirloin steak dinner with dessert was $5.25 at the motel's restaurant, where a sign says: "Open 25 hours a day."

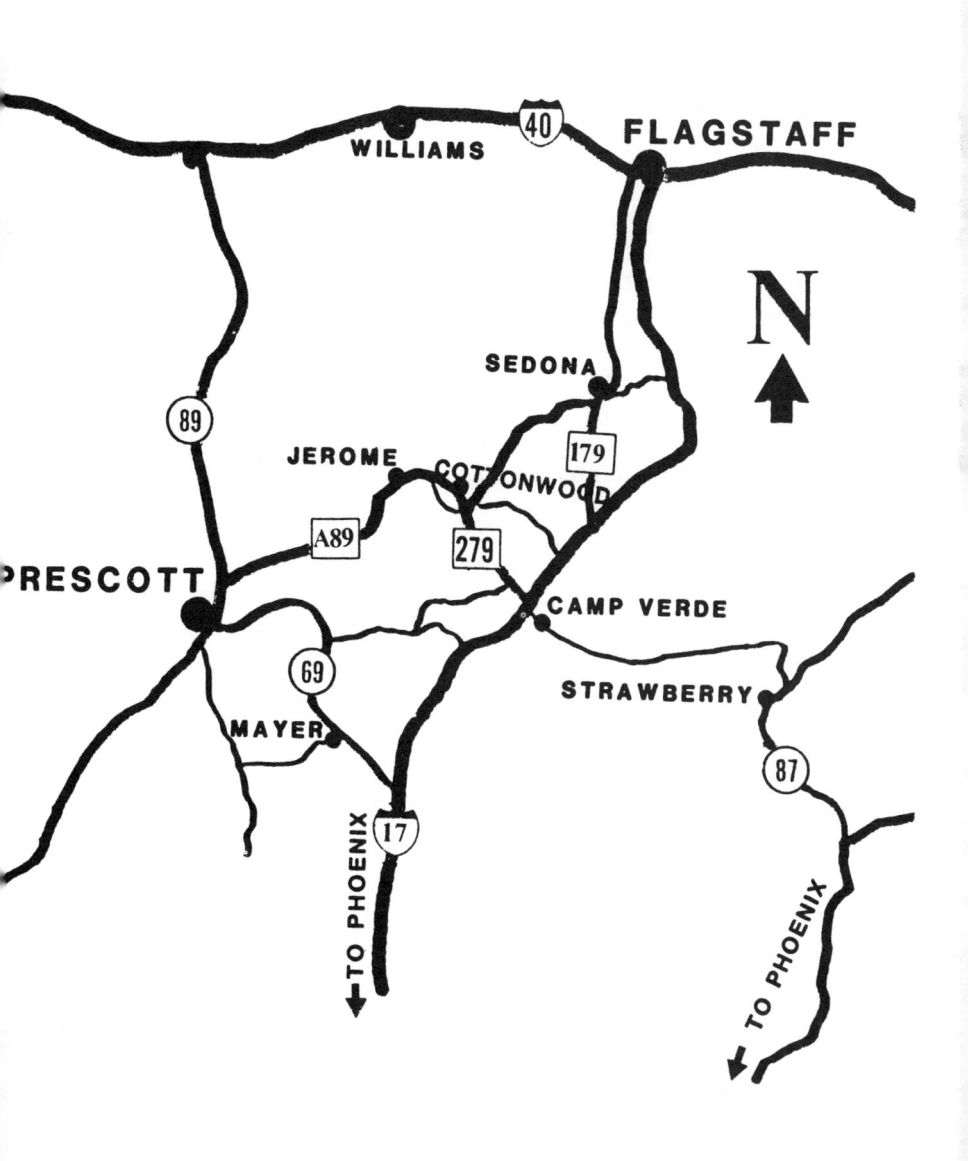

MID-CENTRAL

Map of Mid-Central Arizona

STRAWBERRY
and Arizona's oldest school house

Residents in this small town—tucked beneath the Mogollon Rim—have a propensity for strawberries.

That's understandable. The very name holds a certain charm.

Besides, the place was so named by early settlers because of wild strawberries that grew in the area.

Businesses, rightfully, capitalize on the name. There is a Strawberry Shortcake Restaurant, Strawberry Hill cabins and a Strawberry Market.

Strawberry motifs are used on dishes and even wallpaper in home decor. For that matter, breakfast entrees—in season—at the Strawberry Lodge arrive complete with a juicy, plump strawberry. It's a touch that does not go unnoticed by diners.

There are other strawberry tangents. In circulation—and seen as far as the Phoenix area, are bumper stickers—"I'd Rather Be In Strawberry, Az." How's that for pride in a community?

Despite all this Strawberry fanfare, visitors find a bigger attraction. It's the scenery, the clean air, rustic atmosphere and the pine-scent that wafts in the breeze amid the mountains and peaceful valleys.

Strawberry, in August 1985, celebrated the centennial for the Strawberry School House, built in 1885 along what is now Fossil Creek Road.

The school house brings up a claim to fame for the small but growing community. The historic building is touted as "the oldest, still standing school house in Arizona."

A marker at the site notes that the "log cabin was put up in a single day by a community log-raising party in autumn 1885" and that it was "nicely finished with wallpaper and wainscoting, and well supplied with manufactured desks and blackboards."

Dorothy Ferguson, long time resident here, reports the building was used as a school house until 1916. The long abandoned building was saved in 1961 through efforts of local citizens and later restored. Today it is owned by the Arizona Historical Society, Ferguson said.

The school house, complete with artifacts, is open in spring and summer months on weekends and holidays from 12 noon to 4 p.m.

Strawberry and neighboring Pine, three miles away, are closely linked. The unincorporated communities in Gila County are

Old Strawberry School House—touted as the oldest standing school house in Arizona

jointly served by the Pine and Strawberry Chamber of Commerce, and the Pine and Strawberry Fire Department. Both communities are growing as a vacation and retirement center. The chamber of commerce tags permanent population of the area as up to 2500. The influx of tourists swells that figure, however. Strawberry, too, has many fine mountain homes and construction is continuing.

A post office, established in Strawberry in December 1886 was discontinued on December 31, 1904. Pine, 15 miles from Payson has a post office.

Strawberry at 6047 feet, is a fun place to visit, explore or serve as an anchor place to visit other scenic spots in the Mogollon Rim Country.

A sign near the Strawberry Market directs to "The Hock Crockery" 50 yards away. Pottery and stain glass items are made at the shop.

In our second story room at the Strawberry Lodge the fireplace, set for a ready fire, was not needed on a July visit. The room's balcony offered a quiet place to relax in a cool breeze. At night, a summer rain storm added another pleasant note.

Television, radio and phones noticeably absent in the lodge rooms, added to the scenario. Jean Turner, who with her husband, Dick, are veteran lodge owners, said many patrons view the lodge as a "get-away" place even from television and radio.

A New York steak dinner was relished in the lodge dining room, where decor featured a grandfather clock, mountain scene pictures, big game trophies and a flagstone-fronted fireplace.

Strawberry may be reached by Payson and continuing on State 87 some 18 miles. A second approach, and our choice, is via I-17 and a back-way route through eye-catching country to Strawberry.

And, more about strawberry-related items. Some shoppers take home packages of Strawberry Tea purchased at "The Elegant Hen Shop" at the Windmill Corner building.

Strawberry does offer a change of pace.

Commanding officer's house at Fort Verde State Historic Park

CAMP VERDE
farms, fort and an ancient apartment house

This old town of Camp Verde in the lush Verde Valley historically combines the military, ancient cliff dwellings and a ranching-themed heritage.

The result is interest-packed sightseeing for visitors in this town, some 86 miles north of Phoenix.

The approach off I-17 in Yavapai County into Camp Verde, marked with tall shade trees and sprawling farms, veers into the small town's business district.

Historically, Camp Verde began in 1865 when settlers entered the valley from Prescott seeking a place to settle and farm. They located near the confluence of Clear Creek and the Verde River, about four miles from today's town.

Settlers built a crude dam and diverted water for crops. When Indians raided Verde Valley fields for corn, settlers called on the army.

The military post, in 1865, overlooked farms at West Clear Creek. The next camp, named "Lincoln," was one mile north of the present fort. Today's old Fort Verde, now a state historic park in the heart of town, was built 1871-73.

When the threat of Indian attacks was over, the fort became less important. It was abandoned in 1891 to the Department of Interior and later sold at public auction.

Local citizens began a museum in the adjutant's building and, in 1970, donated several buildings to create the state historic park. It was placed on the National Register of Historic Places in 1971.

The fort is open to the public daily from about mid-March to mid-October, closed on Tuesdays and Wednesdays during other times. A nominal fee is charged for persons 18 and over.

Visitors may view old military uniforms with bright gold braid, guns and other artifacts. Museum wood floors crack and snap with age, beneath footsteps.

Within a short drive, Montezuma Castle, a 20-room "apartment house," occupied between 1100 and 1400 A.D. cast a visitor's fancy into the realm of antiquity. A small entrance fee is required at the national monument and sightseers can sit on benches to contemplate the life of Indian cliff dwellers.

An interesting trail meanders not far from Beaver Creek. Tall sycamores, velvet ash, western soapberry and walnut trees add complementing beauty to prehistoric dwellings in the limestone

Old Clear Creek church, finished in 1903, restored by Camp Verde Historical Society

Ancient Montezuma's Castle in Camp Verde area

cliff.

Montezuma Well is a separate unit of the National Monument, 9.5 miles from the castle. The area contains a large limestone sink with water that reportedly flows out at the rate of 1.5 million gallons a day.

Hardy people can walk down the canyon to the well sink, but that includes 101 steps, a bit tough for some to climb out.

The unincorporated Camp Verde offers two motels, restaurants and a variety of interesting shops such as the White Hills Indian Arts shop and the Skull Valley Stitching Post.

Just off I-17, the Yavapai-Apache Visitors Activity Center, operated in conjunction with the National Park Service, is a must-see. The impressive structure, the target of many cameras, is near the freeway on Montezuma Castle Road.

No first-time visit at Camp Verde would be complete without a visit to the old Clear Creek Church, now beautifully restored by the Camp Verde Historical Society.

COTTONWOOD
modern Old West town!

As Arizona's little towns go, Cottonwood isn't very little. Still, it offers a welcome change of pace to spend a night in this locale.

Our viewpoint literally was lofty. Overnight accommodations were at the comfortable View Motel, atop a hill that offered a splendid view of Cottonwood and the Verde Valley. The valley along the Verde River is some 60 miles long and 40 miles wide. And, the climate is generally mild.

Our first visit here was on a hot July night, and our travel party had toured through the rugged Schnebly Hill country, coasting into Sedona.

One of Cottonwood's stellar features for the casual observer must be the old shade, sometimes arching above the streets.

Cottonwood was named for the many cottonwood trees along the Verde River. It was a farm settlement in the late 1870s. Campfires often burned in the old wagon grounds under the big trees in a wash extending near the Verde River. A post office was established in 1879, and, of course, the name was Cottonwood.

Today there are good-sized, modern shopping centers, plazas and professional offices. Cottonwood's oldest cemetery faces main street, the archway dates proclaiming 1878 to 1938.

A street in Old Town Cottonwood

Shaded retreat at Dead Horse Ranch State Park

Dinner on both visits was at the White Horse Inn, where the menu featured entrees at modest prices. Good, too! There are several restaurants and motels from which to choose.

Old Town in Cottonwood shares in attracting business with shopping centers. The quaint place proved a pleasant surprise, affording visitors with the ambience of an old western downtown street.

Visitors find it fascinating to browse among the some 50 shops, including the Closet Antique and Country Crafts, the Old Town Cottonwood Bakery, Buck Jones Leather Store, the Cottonwood Drug Store, to name a few.

Near the start of Old Town on Main Street, all apart from the main business section, is the Cottonwood Community Center, built in 1939 as the Cottonwood Community Club House. Nearby are the Cottonwood Police Department, Recreation Center and Victory Chapel.

Cottonwood boasts the Marcus Lawrence Hospital and Mingus Mountain High School that serve the north end of Verde Valley, and the town is the home of the longstanding *Verde Independent* newspaper.

Before leaving on the next lap of travel, we visited Dead Horse Ranch State Park, a beautiful area developed for picnicking and camping near the Verde River. Domestic ducks ply the lagoon and the Questa Pine Seed Orchard, established in 1977, is unusual.

At the ranger station, visitors can pay the small fee for picknicking and camping, and learn about facilities. There are 45 campsites, all furnished with water and electricity. Twenty-six picnic tables and grills have been placed among the mesquite trees. There is one large group-use ramada.

Tall cottonwoods along the Verde River provide prime nesting area for many species of birds. The state park is reached by a turn off main street.

As a sidebar trip, there is nearby Tuzigoot National Monument, a prehistoric town built by Indians between 1125 and 1400 A.D. The reconstructed ruins rise against the skyline like an Egyptian pyramid.

And, of course, there is old Jerome, a remnant of an old mining camp on Cleopatra Hill only a few miles away.

Tuzigoot National Monument, a reminder of Sinaguan village—centuries old

Hotel Connor, vintage 1892, in Jerome

JEROME
clinging to the hillside!

The "1892" inscription on faded bricks topping the corner facade at the Hotel Connor sets the stage. And from a window above "The Spirit Room Bar," a curtain stirred in the morning breeze.

Obviously, the hotel would have character. For a night in the town where mining once boomed and burst, visitors wanted the unusual. They got it.

At the hotel, reservations were checked in the Spirit Room Bar. The juke box droned as bar patrons gathered for Friday afternoon fun. A Japanese man aimed his camera at a buddy beaming at the bar with beer in hand.

Room assignments received, guests lugged suitcases and assorted gear up the 28 steps. Not all rooms had private baths, but advanced room reservations had staked out claims for rooms with those facilities.

One room was papered colorfully in flower and bird patterns, and bedspreads were purple. Clean sheets and pillowcases marked the comfortable beds, but there was no television, radio or phone.

The red curtain billowed in a refreshing April breeze. Resting in an old chair, a guest could easily reflect on the town's history.

Earlier in the day, however, tourists were plying the streets, sightseeing, wielding cameras. The old buildings in the former mining town that somehow survived its heyday, combines with spectacular scenery. The combination is a photographer's delight.

Shops boasted jewelry, copper, antiques, brass, pottery, clothing and paintings.

A sidewalk bench beside The Copper Country Fudge Shop offered a chance to rest. The distant scenery from that vantage point is spectacular—a panorama of Red Rock Country with the San Francisco Peaks in the Flagstaff distance.

Lunchtime prompted guests to enter the Candy Kitchen, established in 1952. Oilcloth-covered tables added whimsey and color as did the 48-star U.S. flag adorning one wall.

As for Jerome's history, large-scale mining got underway in the 1880s with the United Verde Copper Co., and decades later Phelps Dodge took over mining activity here. In Jerome's heyday, there were 15,000 people living here, but after mining closed down, there was a mass exodus. The place, however, never became a real ghost town.

Sightseeing is a must to absorb the history in this old town that clutches to the slopes of Cleopatra Hill. A good place to start is at the Jerome Historical Society's Mine Museum and gift shop at 200 Main St.

Elsewhere, there is the "Little Daisy Hotel," built in 1918, primarily to house workers at the Little Daisy Mine. And, it is important to see the Douglas Mansion with its many exhibits in the Jerome State Historical Park. Built in 1916, the mansion was once the home of James S. Douglas, prominent in the mining industry of Jerome.

In 1962, the mansion was donated to the Arizona State Parks Board and opened to the public in 1965. It houses a wealth of history about the old mining town.

Information describes how geological faults and mine tunneling aggravated by blastings in 1924 caused some buildings to shift. Some were torn down and replaced.

Jerome is along U.S. Alt. 89 between Prescott and Cottonwood.

Certainly Arizona travel is not complete without a sightseeing stanza in fascinating Jerome. There is no place in Arizona quite like it. Jerome must be experienced to be believed.

Douglas Mansion now open to public in Jerome

MAYER
where it's easy to make friends!

The people and places in this old town, anchored more than 100 years ago near Big Bug Creek, blend into a fascinating montage.

The rural community today nestles in the Bradshaw foothills along State 69, eight miles northwest of Interstate 17.

The fascination includes landmark buildings like the Olde White House Hotel, built around 1903. Although the welcome mat is no longer out to the general public, the two-story structure bespeaks regally of earlier times.

Visitors, attracted by its stance and atmosphere, aim cameras at the old hostelry where Governor Hunt is said to have slept and Tom Mix partook of its hospitality.

It was in 1881 that Joseph Mayer rode into Big Bug Station as Mayer was first known. He built a home and new station along Big Bug Creek that runs through the town.

Time brought progress. Mayer added a livery station and restaurant. Various mines opened and big ranches developed at the area. His wife, Sarah Belle Mayer, became the first postmaster in 1884.

* * * * *

In 1983, an old building along Central was scene of the Mayer Elder Center. Hot meals were served there five days a week by the Senior Opportunity Service.

A sign out front told the sentiment of Mayer seniors: "Onward Ever, Backward Never."

Across the street is a building once housing the Mayer State Bank. It was the residence of Frank Polk, sculptor of authentic western life and a member of Cowboy Artists of America.

Polk labeled himself an old cowboy, stating he rode broncs in Prescott and "rodeoed" many years. He makes models for molds that are cast in bronze. His autobiographical book is called *F-F-F Frank Polk.*

Polk had lived in Mayer since 1971, but his residency dates earlier.

"I went to school here as a kid," he said, "I live here because I like it here. I don't like a big place."

* * * * *

Olde White House Hotel, built around 1903, is Mayer landmark

The Mayer Public Library, a solar-heated building constructed in 1976, is focus of community pride.

Head librarian Joyce Segner was assisted by volunteers. Besides a small assistance received from Yavapai County, contributions come through memorials, baked food, rummage, sale of books and house plants.

Library volunteer Betty Daugherty lived in nearby Spring Valley. She was also a volunteer firefighter.

Daugherty, wearing a pager (beeper) is on call for emergency services. If a call comes in while serving at the library, she closes the door and posts a sign, "Emergency, Librarian on fire call. Will return."

Townspeople understand.

* * * * *

The town, 25 miles from Prescott, was unincorporated and served by Yavapai County.

The town had a 10-unit motel, the Duncan Oak Hills with restaurant, plus the C & C Restaurant, schools, four churches, two food stores, antique shops and other businesses.

* * * * *

Mel and Lola Crouch, formerly of Glendale, have lived full-time in their home on Stage Coach Road since 1960.

"I was raised in a little town. It is easy to make friends," Crouch said. "To make close friends you have to get out and meet people."

The two helped organize the Mayer Community Church and enjoy bridge games. Other community socials included weekly bingo and fish dinner events.

Crouch considers the climate the "best in Arizona." Nights are quiet.

"Sometimes you can hear the coyotes howl," Lola Crouch added.

* * * * *

On a windswept hillside out of town lies the old Mayer Cemetery with its blossoming wild verbenas.

The story goes that a freighter party long ago stopped to camp for the night and was massacred by Indians. The victims were buried on the site, giving the cemetery a premature beginning.

Former Mayer hotel in downtown Mayer

*Mexican goldpoppies in riotous bloom at
Organ Pipe National Monument*

INDEX of PLACE NAMES

A
Ajo 90-94
Alpine 44-45, 47, 55
Apache Forest 48
Apache Leap 57
Arizona Strip 9-10
Ash Fork 21-23

B
Bear Canyon 49
Beaver Creek 114
Benson 72-75
Big Bug Creek 121
Big Sandy River 99
Bill Williams Mt. & River 18
Bisbee 76-79
Black Canyon Creek 41-42
Black Mesa 13
Black Mountains 101
Bowie 66-68
Boyce Thompson SW Arboretum 57-59
Bradshaw Mtns. 121
Brewery Gulch 76, 79
Buckskin Wash 41
Bullhead City 101-102

C
Cameron 15-17
Camp Verde 113-115
Cataract Lake 18
Chambers 33-35
Chase Creek 54-55
Chiricahua Monument 67
Clear Creek 113, 114
Cleopatra Hill 118
Clifton 52-56
Cochise 69-71
Coconino Forest 23
Colorado River 12-14, 101-104
Colorado River Indian Res. 103-105
Coronado Trail, 44-46, 48-50, 52, 55
Cottonwood 116-118

D-E
Davis Dam 101
Dead Horse Ranch Park 117, 120
Dogtown Lakes 18-20
Dripping Springs Hills 62
Eagle Creek 48-50
Echo Cliffs 14

F
First Mesa 27
Flagstaff 14
Ft. Bowie 66-67
Ft. Crittendon 85
Ft. Defiance 30-32
Ft. Tyson 108
Ft. Verde State Park 113-114
Fredonia 9-11

G
Galiuro Mts. 63
Gatlin Ruins 89
Gila Bend 87-89
Gila River 60, 87
Gleeson 75
Glen Canyon Bridge 14
Glen Canyon Dam 12-13
Grand Canyon 15, 18
Grand Canyon Caverns 25
Grand Canyon Deer Farm 19

H
Hannagan Meadow 46-47
Hardyville 101
Hassayampa River 96-97
Heber 41-42
Holbrook 38
Honeymoon 48-50
Hopi Reservation 27-28
Huachuca Mtns. 80

I-K
Iron Mtn. 57
Jerome 118-120
Jerome State Historic Park 120
Kaibab 10
Kaibab Forest 23
Kaibab Lake 18
Keams Canyon 27
Kearny 60-62
Kingman 99

L
Lake Havasu City 102
Lake Powell 12-14
Laughlin, NV 101
Little Colorado River 15-17, 37
Lowell 78
Luna Lake 45
Lyman's Lake 37

M
Mammoth 63-64
Maps—North Central 8
    Northeast 26
    East 43
    Southeast 65
    Southwest 86
    West 95
    Mid-Central 109
Mayer 121-124
Mile-Hi Preserve 81-82
Mineral Creek 60
Mogollon Rim 40-42, 46, 110, 112
Mohave Lake 101
Montezuma's Castle 114-115
Montezuma's Well 115
Morenci 51-52, 55
Mule Gulch/Pass 76

N-O
Navajo Generating Station 13
Navajo Res. 13-17, 29-33
Newspaper Rock 34-35
Nogales 83
Oraibi 27-28
Organ Pipe Cactus N. M. 89, 93
Overgaard 41-42

P
Page 12-14
Painted Desert 14-15, 35
Painted Rocks Dam/Park 89
Parker 101, 103-105
Parker Dam 103-104
Patagonia 83-85
Patagonia Lake 83
Patagonia-Sonoita Creek
    Sanctuary 83-85
Peach Springs 25
Pearce 75
Petrified Forest 33-35
Picket Post Mtn. 57-59
Pine 112
Pipe Springs 11
Puerco River 33

Q-R
Quartzsite 106-108
Questa Pine Seed Orchard 117-118
Rainbow Bridge 12
Rainbow Forest 35
Ramsey Canyon 80-82
Ray 60-61
Route 66—18, 21, 22, 24-25

S
St. Johns 36-37
St. Michael's 31-32
San Francisco Peaks 27
San Francisco River 54-55
San Jose 78
San Manuel 63
San Pedro River 60
San Pedro Valley 63
Schnebly Hill 116
Second Mesa 27-28
Sedona 116
Seligman 24-25
Signal 100
Sitgreaves Forest 44-45, 48
Snowflake 38-40
Sonoita 83
Sonoita Creek 83
Spring Valley 122
Steamboat Rock 9
Strawberry 110-112
Superior 57-60
Sycamore Canyon 18

T
Third Mesa 27
Thompson (Boyce)
    SW Arboretum 57-59
Tombstone 75, 83
Tombstone Canyon 76
Tonto Forest 57
Tortilla Mountains 62
Tuba City 27
Tuzigoot Nat'l Mon. 118
Tyson's Wells 108

V-Z
Verde River 113, 116-118
Verde Valley 113, 116-117
Wahweap 12, 14
Walnut Creek 25
Warren 78
White Horse Lake 18
Wickenburg 96-98
Wikieup 99-100
Willcox 69
Williams 18-20
Williams, Bill (Mtn. & River) 18
Window Rock 29-32
Winkelman 60
Winslow 27
Wonderland of Rocks 67

Order from your book dealer or direct from publisher.

▪▪▪▪▪▪▪▪▪▪▪▪▪ ORDER BLANK ▪▪▪▪▪▪

Golden West Publishers

4113 N. Longview Ave.,
Phoenix, AZ 85014

Please ship the following books:

- _____ Arizona Adventure ($5.00)
- _____ Arizona Cook Book ($3.50)
- _____ Arizona Hideaways ($4.50)
- _____ Arizona Museums ($5.00)
- _____ Arizona—Off the Beaten Path ($4.50)
- _____ Arizona Outdoor Guide ($5.00)
- _____ California Favorites Cook Book ($3.50)
- _____ Chili-Lovers' Cook Book ($3.50)
- _____ Citrus Recipes ($3.50)
- _____ Cowboy Slang ($5.00)
- _____ Explore Arizona ($5.00)
- _____ Fools' Gold (Lost Dutchman Mine) ($5.00)
- _____ Ghost Towns in Arizona ($4.50)
- _____ Greater Phoenix Street Maps Book ($4.00)
- _____ How to Succeed in Selling Real Estate ($3.50)
- _____ In Old Arizona ($5.00)
- _____ Mexican Cook Book ($5.00)

I enclose $ _____ (including $1 per order postage, handling).

Name _____

Address _____

City _____ State _____ Zip _____

This order blank may be photo copied

Books from Golden West Publishers

Read of the daring deeds and exploits of Wyatt Earp, Buckey O'Neill, the Rough Riders, Arizona Rangers, cowboys, Power brothers shootout, notorious Tom Horn, Pleasant Valley wars, "first" American revolution—action-packed true tales of early Arizona! *Arizona Adventure (by Marshall Trimble), 160 pages... $5.00.*

The lost hopes, the lost lives—the lost gold! Facts, myths and legends of the Lost Dutchman Gold Mine and the Superstition Mountains. Told by a geologist who was there! *Fools' Gold (by Robert Sikorsky), 144 pages... $5.00.*

Take the back roads to and thru Arizona's natural wonders—Canyon de Chelly, Wonderland of Rocks, Monument Valley, Rainbow Bridge, Four Peaks, Swift Trail, Alamo La' Virgin River Gorge, Palm Canyon, Red Rc Country! *Arizona—off the beaten path! (by Thelma Heatwole), 144 pages... $4.50.*

Plants, animals, rocks, minerals, geologic history, natural environments, landforms, resources, national forests and outdoor survival—with maps, photographs, drawings, charts, index. *Arizona Outdoor Guide (by Ernest E. Snyder), 126 pages ... $5.00*

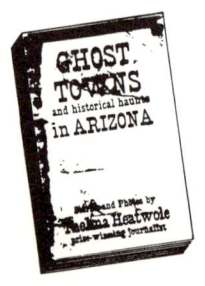

Visit the silver cities of Arizona's golden past with this prize-winning reporter-photographer. Come along to the towns whose heydays were once wild and wicked! See crumbling adobe walls, old mines, cemeteries, cabins and castles. *Ghost Towns and Historical Haunts in Arizona (by Thelma Heatwole), 144 pages... $4.50.*

Discover the Arizona that most tourists never see! Explore caves, ghost towns, ruins, lava tubes, ice caves, cliff dwellings! Sixty fabulous places, sixty full-page maps! *Explore Arizona! (by Rick Harris) 128 pages... $5.00.*